LIBERTY AND LAW

UNDER

FEDERATIVE GOVERNMENT.

BY

BRITTON A. HILL.

PHILADELPHIA:
J. B. LIPPINCOTT & CO.
1874.

LIPPINCOTT'S PRESS,
PHILADELPHIA.

PREFACE.

In the course of thirty-five years' practice of the law, I have had many opportunities to observe the operations of our federative form of government, and of our different State constitutions and laws, upon the welfare, rights, and liberties of the citizens for whose benefit they were organized.

A careful study has convinced me that the main danger to the permanence of our federative republican institutions lies, firstly, in an originally deficient machinery of State and federal organization; and secondly, in a misconception on the part of our governments, State and federal, of their full duties under the law. To the former defect we owe the outbreak of the late war, which under a properly constructed machinery of State and federative governments would never have occurred; to the latter we owe the growth of those powerful monopolies that, in conjunction with ignorance and impurity,—alternately supporting and deriving support from these,—threaten every form of liberty that has grown dear to us.

The demoralization consequent upon the late war has hastened the general recognition of this latter defect in our political organization, by developing the powers of those monopolies in our midst to an extent which makes the danger threatened by them directly perceptible to every citizen.

It would have been useless at any previous period in our history to expose these sores on our political body and prescribe their cure. But I think the time has come now when the minds of the people are ripe for a thorough reorganization of our State and federative governments, leaving the grand idea of their founders untouched in the main, but supplying the elements that are needed in order to remove the disorders which must otherwise undermine their life.

It may be objected that it is too bold a task to sketch even the mere outlines of such a reorganization, and I readily concede that no higher one can engage the mind of man than to delineate such a plan through all its features, State, federal, and International. Nor can I say anything in deprecation, except that the thought of this work has engaged the best part of my life, and accompanied me throughout all my experience of legal practice and a careful study of civilizations, of hygiene, and past and contemporary history.

If, however, I fail in presenting such a plan in its

completeness of organization under constitutional and codified systems of laws, I can only hope that others following in the same direction with greater ability will accomplish this more perfectly than I have done. With a well-grounded belief in the capacity of the human race for an unlimited advance in government, morality, law, art, science, and all other means whereby the miseries, crimes, follies, and evils of life may be lessened, and its happiness increased as much as possible by wise and just systems of laws, bearing equally upon all, I send this work forth to the people, to plead the cause of the oppressed, and to break down the despotic systems and monopolies that now fortify and increase the power of the oppressors.

BRITTON A. HILL.

ST. LOUIS, August, 1873.

CONTENTS.

LIBERTY AND LAW.

I. PUBLIC HYGIENE.

II. PUBLIC EDUCATION.

INTERCOMMUNICATION BY THE PRESS.

DOMESTIC RELATIONS.

INTRODUCTION.

In considering the history of all governments heretofore established by man, the student feels disheartened to meet everywhere inadequateness and failure. From the earliest beginning of history, when, under a patriarchal form of rule, men first were led to the conception of a government of law, through all the various forms of government that have since arisen and been swept away, the common result of disappointment and failure stares him everywhere in the face, most discouragingly in the oldest organized countries of the earth, in China, Persia, Egypt, and India, where despotism rules so absolutely that its principal check is the dagger of the assassin ; the aspect is, nevertheless, sad enough even in the younger civilizations of Europe, and it is only in our own country that, by the establishment of a federative republic, a hopeful state of things has finally been brought about, which is constantly threatened, however, by the growth of various forms of despotism within and around it.

It cannot but prove instructive to examine into the causes of this universal previous disappointment, and to discover the reason why all former attempts at the establishment of adequate governments of law have proved failures, and what it was in their organizations that became the elements of their destruction, or their perversion to the purposes of tyranny.

If it appears that these destroying elements were in all cases some forms of special prerogatives conferred upon a part of the people to the exclusion of all others, either a prerogative of caste, of hierarchy, of exclusive right to rule, or of money-monopoly, we shall be taught to comprehend what measures we ourselves require to ward off the dangers that threaten in the future, and the fate that has overtaken all other governments and people in the past.

Again, if it shall appear that their inadequateness had its cause always in a neglect to provide for the utmost development of all the faculties of mind and body of all citizens, thus fostering ignorance, impurity, and vice to assist the prerogative elements in their movement to crush the happiness, rights, and liberties of the people, we shall be able to realize more effectively the necessity of protecting every citizen in his threefold functions as a member of the physical world, as a member of the spiritual-intellectual world, and as a member of the social state, against all the encroachments and injuries to which he may be exposed.

The hierarchical-caste element, which overthrew the Mosaic fabric of government, we, under our constitution, which recognizes no religion of any kind, but leaves each one to worship God according to the dictates of his own conscience, need not fear nor legislate against; but the despotism of any part of the governmental power, be it the legislative, the executive, the judicial, or merely the despotism of a majority under unconstitutional and unjust laws, must certainly be avoided by the most effective checks; the deadly rule of impurity, ignorance, and vice we must abolish altogether, and we must crush the old and new tyrannies that are growing up in our midst, and which in all free states and cities have, at all times and everywhere, in the Greek as well as in the Italian republics, been most fatal, because most insidious: the tyrannies of money-power and of monopolies.

No state of ancient or modern times has ever made this its definite aim and object, and the neglect to rise to this high and truly rational view of the purpose of government sufficiently accounts for the numberless disheartening failures. If at times great thinkers, like Plato and Confucius in the old world, and Hegel and others in the modern world, have tried to grasp this problem, at least theoretically, the result has been in the former cases simply a collection of idealistic dogmatic notions, having no connection with the actual relation between men under a government of law; and in the case of the latter, an arbitrary vindication of existing forms without regard to their inherent justice or sufficiency. Unsuccessful as have been the great legislators of antiquity, the philosophers that should have pointed out the defects in their legislation, and the remedies, only wandered still farther astray.

The problem now submitted to American statesmen is to discover how to perfect the wise creation of *our* great legislators,—of Washington, Jefferson, Adams, Henry, Madison, Franklin, Hamilton, and others,—by adding to it all that a strictly philosophical comprehension of their work may demand, regardless of any traditional superstition that may have influenced them in the construction of our form of government.

In the present work I purpose to make an attempt in this direction, and to supplement our State and federal codes by the measures necessary to perfect them, in order that, by removing existing evils and abuses, they may successfully withstand all the dangers of the future. I do this without prejudice or favor, submitting the needed reforms to the people for their examination and amendment.

In the present book, having first criticised the historical forms of government of previous times, so far as they have any bearing upon ours and teach us the dangers that threaten us, I proceed to announce and justify the true fundamental principles of a State organization generally, and by their analysis to apply them to the actual legislation needed.

Extending this application to the threefold function of man, I show how a representative government, that intends to realize its purpose to its full extent, must establish by positive legislation—1, a complete system of sanitary laws to protect the bodies of its citizens against all impurities and disease, the breeders of misery and crime; 2, a complete system of education, extending to every function of the mind and body, to protect the intellectual culture of its citizens against the evil influences of ignorance and superstition in all forms, and against pauperism, by providing each one with the means of making a livelihood; and 3, a complete system of intercommunication between men, whereby to take from out of the despotic influence of money, and all other monopolies, the terrible power which they so long have wielded to oppress the people, and to exercise that power, through a State organization and federation, for the benefit, not for the injury, of the people.

In a subsequent work I purpose to develop the application of those fundamental principles as requiring, for the purpose of securing to all men immunity from the unlawful interference of others—1st, a code of laws and a constitution for each State; 2d, a political constitution for the federative republic of all the States; and 3d, an international constitution for all the states of the world, as they may gradually and one after another see the wisdom of adopting such a legal international form of government, if it be practicable, as I believe it to be.

While the code of laws will point out the civil and criminal legislation needed, the constitution will be shown to demand a synthetical form, wherein alone the double requirement of all government—1st, that it should have absolute power to carry out all its purposes and laws for the good and happiness of all; and 2d, that it should be absolutely checked in the exercise of that power whenever attempted to be wielded in an unjust and improper way—can, 3d, be united in its character of a federative republic. This triune characteristic, entering all the functions of the State organization, will necessarily also be applied to them, separating the whole organization primarily into legislative, judicial, and executive departments, and again each of these departments into three separate bodies. Thus, the legislature will be composed of three houses, one representing the people at large, the second one all property-owners, and the third one the academical force of the State; the executive also will be composed of a council of three persons instead of one man, and the federative and State judiciary will be separated into three different courts of divided and special functions.

This conception of a triple legislation may at first appear novel, but suffrage, in order to be truly universal, should embrace all the fundamental elements of power in the State, so as to represent all the people of the State in their triune powers of individuality, of wealth, and of knowledge. Each of these powers should be harmoniously exercised to secure the common good and happiness of all, without creating any prerogative caste, class, or monopoly, leaving the preferment of competitors free and open to all through the schools to be established in each State for the acquisition of knowledge, morality, wealth, and true individuality.

Thus each person may become the architect of his own fortunes, under the wise universal protection and aid of a government of law, having one common object, the permanent good and happiness of each citizen, and the people may come to regard the State as a friend, and the rule of law as the only safeguard for the preservation of liberty under the forms of representative federative systems of government.

In the organization of the judicial department of the federal republic, I propose to prevent future wars between the States, and restore all the States to a just and equal sovereignty under the law, by organizing as a permanent safeguard an inter-state-national judicial tribunal, whose functions shall be to determine all controversies between the federative States, between one or more States and the federal government, and between the citizens of any State and the federal or State governments; in which court any State or the federal government may be sued, and suffer judgment by due course of law or equity.

Two other federal judicial tribunals, of separate, distinct jurisdictions over all other causes and proceedings provided for in the code of the federative government, should be organized, with an appeal in important causes to the Supreme Inter-state-national Court.

I shall finally recommend the organization, by the consent of several or all of the civilized nations of the world, of an international judicial tribunal for the legal settlement of all controversies between states, nations, kingdoms, and empires; providing for the selection of a judicial officer from each nation that enters this international federation, and to form a court to settle all disputes and controversies between nations; to render judgment on trial before this international court; and to regulate and adjust all cases of controversies between the same parties in the interchange of moneyed values, and the settlement of balances between all parts of the said international federation, by the organization of an international clearing-house under the jurisdiction and control of such court.

Thus, from the lowest function of government, to provide for the direct security and sanitary welfare of each citizen, my work will trace its duties to the highest in the creation of an international court, which may remove all just causes of war between the federated nations, and realize the common wish of all good men by the maintenance of universal peace.

In this age, when the forces of heat and electricity, manifested in the telegraph and the steam-power, have brought the people of the world into such near contact and direct communication with each other that the welfare of each individual is more intimately connected with that of his fellow-men than ever before, when even the long locked-up civilization of Japan opens itself to the influence of our own, and seeks to establish our own imperfect systems of law, of education, and of money of divers kinds; it is clearly our duty to raise our energies to a level with the spirit of the age, and discover, if we can, a truly universal system of federative government, under wise, equal, just, harmonious, and all-embracing laws, that shall be applicable to all races, nations, castes, and men that may be subjected to its influence, and which may effectually secure to one and all, for all time to come, the greatest good, happiness, morality, wisdom, and perfection that humanity is capable of attaining.

LIBERTY AND LAW.

LIBERTY AND LAW.

CHAPTER I.

THE MOSAIC CODE.

Of all the attempts of antiquity to establish a government that should secure the greatest good, happiness, and wisdom to men, and bear equally upon all persons in the state, the most perfect and successful was the oldest of which we have record, the legislation of Moses.

A Hebrew of the tribe of the Levites, having fled from Egypt into Midian, where he had exiled himself for forty years under the protection of Jethro, a priest, whose daughter he married, Moses conceived there the idea to found a state with a government of law of divine origin; to realize those objects of the greatest good, happiness, and wisdom; and selecting the Hebrews, who had been nomadic tribes for several centuries before their arrival in Egypt, where they had since been enslaved, he hit upon the bold design of emancipating them from servitude and leading them out of Egypt into the land of Canaan, where he purposed to found a government of law that should apply equally to all citizens.

The lawgiver was to be Jehovah, the interpreter

between Jehovah and the people was to be Aaron, the brother of Moses, and the tribe of the Levites, of the family of Moses; and Aaron, was to hold exclusively the office of the priestly order, which under this theocratic form of government was necessarily also the temporal governmental order, for all time to come; whilst out of their order was to be chosen the high-priest or chief magistrate, who was to interpret the will of God to his announced chosen people, with whom he intended to dwell in a tabernacle built for his worship, and wherein the ark of his covenant was to be placed within the veil of his holy temple.

Judges were to be selected from all the tribes, according to their attainments and wisdom, to sit in judgment in all the actions and suits between the people, subject to a final appeal to the high-priest, who was the chief executive officer, civil, judicial, political, and religious, and who, moreover, might be the military leader in time of war. Every tribe regulated its own domestic affairs in all other matters. The whole form of government thus established by Moses was, therefore, that of a federative republic.

With such a great design of a form of government, altogether new for his time, and with a no less wonderfully elaborate code of laws to carry it out, prepared during his forty years of exile in the land of Midian, this hero came down to Lower Egypt at the age of eighty years to deliver his people from bondage, and to found a model government, under the direct protection and rule of Jehovah, whose voice he believed he had heard in the burning bush on Mount Horeb, summoning him to deliver the people whom he had chosen to dwell with on earth, and to govern them by divine laws and authority through the agency of a high-priest.

He delivered them from slavery, led them through the Red Sea, announced to them the divine law from Mount Sinai, purified them by daily instruction for forty years in the desert and the wilderness, approaching the land of Canaan by circuitous routes through a terrible pilgrimage of forty years, that was necessary to renew the race of the Hebrew slaves of Egypt by new men and women born in this desert and wilderness, a new race that might be obedient to the law and inured to the art and hardships of war; and, having accomplished this object, he ascended the height of Pisgah, gazed upon the distant land of Canaan, and died alone on Nebo's lonely mountain, in the land of Moab, where the great lawgiver sleeps in an unknown grave.

The wonderful wisdom of Moses in laying down the fundamental principles of law for the just government of the people was not fully appreciated until some time after his death, when the effects of his system showed its results in the elevation of the Hebrews from the most abject slavery to a condition of comparative freedom and happiness under the government of the high-priest and the judges that administered the law according to the code prepared by Moses.

The government thus established was in its nature

strictly theocratic, and in its character the only one of the kind that has ever been established in the history of mankind; God himself being the leader and king of his chosen people, the priesthood alone holding communion with him in the sacredness of the tabernacle; and yet the people ruling themselves, and organized in the only rational form of government, which is that of a federative republic. For it seems evident that Moses intended originally to confine the communication of the priests with Jehovah in the main to spiritual matters, to elevate their moral nature, and bring them into that direct contact with the fountain of inspiration, which alone can raise man from his degradation and lowliness.

This grand conception of a government derived from God himself, the king of the Hebrews, immortal, invisible, all-powerful, and all-sufficient, gave that people a confidence in their Divine Protector that made them invincible for more than four hundred years.

But this theocracy, though very powerful, was not strong enough to resist the corrupting influences of wealth, luxury, and absolute dominion. The vast difference between the social station and prerogative rights of the priesthood and the people of the other tribes laid the foundation of the monarchy and royal prerogative, which ended in the downfall of the state and the dispersion of the chosen people to the four winds of heaven.

Before such theocratic prerogative power the freedom of the individual Hebrew became a reproach.

The people of the tribes were no longer freemen, but slaves of power and prerogative.

The priesthood, the highest office in the state, from whose ranks the high-priest, the chief ruler, was chosen, being confined to a single tribe, the family of Levi, that family thus became the fountain of all honor, power, and profit in the state. This aristocratic feature in the Mosaic constitution finally destroyed the civil liberties of the Jews and overthrew the state, while the changes made in the Mosaic code by this hierarchy for its self-interest uprooted the morality of the Mosaic law, and thus assisted in the final dispersion and ruin of the chosen people.

In this way the attempt of Moses to organize a state constitution for the realization of the highest good, happiness, and freedom of the people of his race resulted in a failure; and the most admirable attempt to form a state organization, based upon the only true principles of a federative republic, wherein every citizen was to be equally protected in his rights, and raised to the highest standard of excellence by an admirably contrived system of sanitary regulations, and such moral education as the age was capable of, shattered upon the introduction of the hierarchical element in the plan of the republic.

It was by reason of the perpetual conflict introduced by this element in the Mosaic code, between the laws applied to the people and physical nature and the prerogative powers of the priesthood, that the civil fabric of the federative republic continued only about four hundred years, from the conquest of

Palestine in the year 1500 B.C., to the establishment of the Hebrew monarchy in the year 1100 B.C. It was not important to the final failure of the Mosaic code of government whether the high-priest or a king exercised the supreme power; it was this despotic feature of the code itself which eventually, in its results, overthrew the liberties of the people, and expelled them from the land of Judæa, making them wanderers over the earth ever since.

And yet, in despite of the downfall of his political fabric, what a legislator must that man have been who was able to raise tribes that had sunk down to the lowest condition of slavery to a moral consciousness and height, which has kept the Jews a separate organization to this day! All other historical national bodies have perished, only the Jew has survived. Nay, more: having been for the second time cast down to the lowest depth of degradation, expelled from their native country and scattered over the world, the Jews have elevated themselves sheerly by dint of their own moral power and self-consciousness to a position which compels wonder and admiration. It was the Jew that brought to the illiterate Christians of the west, in the Middle Ages, the lore of the Arabians, their mathematics, and their Aristotelian metaphysics; it was the Jew that dictated to them the terms on which to borrow money, and invented for them the system of banking; it was the Jew that thus gradually raised himself to the supreme power of the European world, the money-power, controlling even now the destinies of empires;

and it is the Jew who has finally, in our day, subdued and made subject to one of his representatives, the Baron von Reuter, that same empire of Persia, where his forefathers mourned as captives under the willow-trees and wept by the rivers of Babylon.

CHAPTER II.

THE GREEK REPUBLICS.

In some way or another that same element of a prerogative despotism, which overthrew the Mosaic state, has proved the destruction of every hitherto established form of government. And this of necessity. For the object of a state organization, being to apply laws equally to all citizens, the very conception of a prerogative is at war with the conception of such a state, and must necessarily destroy it and again be destroyed by it. Every political contradiction must die by its very nature.

In the Judæan republic, the most successful of ancient times, it was, as has been shown, the hierarchical element which destroyed the state. The Greek so-called republics are scarcely worthy of political examination. No people had less conception of state organization than that people, which from its own high individual culture needed it indeed least, but, it might also be said, needed it most, as a fitting frame and inclosure for the world of beauty which it produced. For, with a fitting government of law, this marvelously gifted people might have achieved results far more extensive than it did achieve, and saved mankind the centuries of retrogression consequent upon the downfall of all forms of government which followed the irruption of the Huns and Goths into Europe.

But the Greeks had an aversion to all fixed form of government, an aversion as great as that of the Indian tribes of our own country, whose political mode of living has indeed an extraordinary resemblance to that of the early Greeks; Agamemnon, for instance, having about all the power, and not a whit more, of an Indian chief. They could not bring themselves to acknowledge a general government of law in the pride of their individuality, and consequently they perished.

Thus, as the Mosaic government, in its first grand results of raising a tribe of miserable slaves, ignorant, filthy, and lawless in the highest degree, to a condition of remarkable strength, intelligence, and political culture, shows the power, effectiveness, and necessity of a strictly defined state organization, established upon pure principles of reason, so the history of the Greek republics shows us, on the other hand, the negative of all this, and how the most gifted of all people of the earth perished necessarily because it disregarded the need of law.

The opposite of the Jews in all respects; the Greek people had formed itself out of all sorts of elements of humanity; contracting no fixed character, no fixed ties of tribe or nationality, but leaving everything free, youthful, and individual. Their ideal is represented in Achilles, the foremost knight of that age; and as in the knightly period of the Middle Ages the crusades formed the first great bond of union for these individual fighters, so the siege of Troy first combined the Hellenes into one people, but without any definite organization and law, each being his own lawgiver. This disorganized condition lasted for a long time, and in it the first sign of prerogative showed itself as the cities of Greece rose by commerce and trade to importance and power. For a long time the acquisition of more territory by colonization checked the growth of despotism, as it has done and does now in our own country; but the power of money and monopoly, which all trade and commerce, not regulated by wise and just laws, invariably produces, finally asserted itself, and then there arose tyrants in the cities. Moses had purposely prohibited commerce to his own people, and by that measure, as well as by his judicious laws of bankruptcy, made money-despotisms impossible in the state. Sparta was probably the only state in Greece which retained a republican form of government for any length of time under the laws of Lycurgus, who tried to bring about the same result which Moses effected by his prohibition of commerce and his laws of bankruptcy, in introducing and establishing iron as the only allowable money, and prohibiting the sale of property. This virtually excluded the spirit of commerce from Sparta, and thereby checked the development of moneyed monopolies.

All the other cities of Greece changed from republican forms of government to despotisms alternately, the people heeding little their political combination, nor the laws which were to afford them protection, in which unconcern the establishment of slavery as well as the virtual absence of monogamic family life materially assisted. Art, beauty, culture, and individual independence in the enjoyment of these things, absorbed all the attention of the Greek citizen. It was not the law itself, but the tone of voice in which it was announced, the gesture which accompanied its enunciation, that determined its acceptance. A finer modulated tone and more expressive and beautiful gesture of another orator caused to-morrow its repeal.

Nevertheless, no sooner did the Persian ruler approach with his terrific army of millions to crush the world of individual freedom with the weight of Asiatic despotism, than all these reckless, free, gay, and brave young Greeks rushed together as one people, and slew the common enemy in the most momentous conflicts of history.

But the Persian wars, in their effects of increasing the wealth of the Grecian cities, particularly of Athens, by the immense contributions exacted from other places, only increased the evil of money-power and prerogative, making possible the success of so reckless a man as Alcibiades, the Jim

Fisk of his time, and instigating the wars between the various parts of Greece, whereby all of them finally became the prey of Philip of Macedon and his son Alexander, who gave them what they had never had, a fixed government and administration of law. But it was too late, and, like Judæa, Greece fell into the hands of the most powerful of all state organizations of the Old World, the Roman republic.

CHAPTER III.

THE ROMAN REPUBLIC.

If the Greek republics collapsed chiefly from want of any fixed state organization, and from the growth of money- and monopoly-prerogatives, the fall of the Roman republic shows in the most vivid and effective way how the strongest organization is doomed to suffer the same fate from the workings of the latter alone.

Under the old kings a sort of theocratic-despotic form of government held the Roman people together with iron severity. Monogamic as the Hebrews under the code of Moses, it was the violation of the sanctity of matrimony which roused the Roman people under the elder Brutus to expel Tarquin, their last king, and establish a republican form of government, the aristocratic features of which—in that a class of patricians exercised all political power—soon gave way to the constant pressure exercised on it by the populace, until, after many conflicts, the common people succeeded in securing a system of written laws to protect them in their rights and property, besides effecting many other political reforms in the organization of the state for their protection against the encroachments of patrician prerogative. The existence of slavery had been a powerful element in favor of the patricians during this whole period of struggle for equal liberties on the part of the people.

The establishment of these laws,—the twelve tables,—which have been the foundation of all succeeding legislation, and the adoption soon after of the Licinian laws, virtually did away with the last distinctions between patricians and plebeians, and inaugurated the happiest period of the Roman republic. It was then that by an unhappily growing love of war and conquest, which extended the rule of the Roman people gradually over all Italy, Carthage, Greece, Macedon, Palestine, Spain, Gaul, etc., there arose a class of men who, by the acquisition of wealth and military power, laid the foundation for the downfall of the republic. The immense number of provinces subjected in course of time to the Romans made necessary the presence of many vast armies, under ambitious leaders, by the very nature of their profession unfriendly to republican principles, as also an equally dangerous body of tax-collectors, proconsuls, etc., who amassed fabulous sums by their oppressions and extortions, sending to Rome as much as possible, but putting the main part of the plunder into their own pockets.

The whole state organization thus began to fall under the control of a band of robbers, the most colossal in power that has ever held sway, and which maintained its power, as the Tweed band did in New York, by dividing its plunder with the poor classes. Idleness and luxury followed this terrible system of spoliation. The wealthy robbers, the high officials in power, introduced every species of extravagance that could be found under the wide domain of the empire; the poor gathered around the market-places in idleness to pick up their share of the distribution of these "revenues." In vain did Tiberius Gracchus, and Caius, his brother, oppose themselves to the most shameful of these money-monopolies; bribery and corruption had become so general that Jugurtha was able to buy up even the Roman senate. Thirsting now for continuous war as a permanent source of plunder, the Roman people soon started wars among themselves, and civil discord thus became for their ambitious leaders the same step to advancement which foreign conflicts had been. The massacres of Marius and Sulla in Rome made offices vacant for their friends, and filled their hands with money and vast possessions. The slave population, which had been constantly increased in number under this demoralizing state of things, attempted under Spartacus in vain to free itself; Crassus, one of the foremost of the official plunderers, after a terrible struggle terribly suppressed it; while Pompey, another one, won his celebrated victory over the pirates; the ruling principle being, that no minor thieves should be tolerated lest the greater ones of Rome might not get all; until the greatest, but at the same time one of the most gifted and extraordinary of all men of history, Julius Cæsar, succeeded in placing the control of the whole empire, the most powerful of all historical empires, in his own hands and virtually ended the Roman republic.

CHAPTER IV.

THE FEUDAL GOVERNMENTS.

THE Roman republic having crushed all other historical governments, and itself having been crushed by the rise of a military and money-despotism, vast enough to overpower even so powerful a fabric, the civilized people of Europe had all sank into a condition of slavery under the Roman empire, from which they were aroused only when the wild hordes of Asia overran the empire and threw all Europe into a state of political and legal chaos. For miserably as the Romans had contrived the political organization of their republic and empire, they had exhibited a genius for municipal law, which has ever excited the admiration of the legal profession in all countries. Strange that a people so highly advanced in the science of jurisprudence should have understood so little of the science of political government! But with the invasion of Italy by the barbarian hordes all that municipal law, so admirably collected and arranged by Justinian, was as completely swept out of sight as the Roman empire itself, and it was not till the twelfth century that it was re-discovered, since which time it has gradually again asserted its influence, more or less, upon the jurisprudence of modern Europe.

But meanwhile there grew up from the fifth to the tenth centuries, in varying forms, over France, Germany, England, Aragon, and part of Italy, the Asiatic system of feudal rule and law which still partly holds its own in England, though it has been recently abolished in Japan; a system that, whatever advantage it had over the centralized despotism of Rome, by disintegrating the one-man power of imperial rule, still retained the most essential features of despotism, in establishing hereditary prerogatives of a favored class, or aristocracies of birth, which the weakness of the kings under that system found it impossible to check. Noted warriors were endowed with benefices, or fiefs, of large tracts of land, which they endeavored, and generally successfully, to secure permanently to their families, while governors of provinces similarly contrived to make their power hereditary. Gradually these men assumed titles according to their several functions, and thus arose the numerous classes of dukes, counts, marquises, margraves, barons, etc., which figured so extensively in the Middle Ages, and laid the foundation of that aristocracy of birth whose members, sprung from the lowest hordes of savages, finally claimed to be God-chosen superiors of the more honest but poorer people, and thereby established the monarchical tyrannies in the various countries of Europe.

Compared with the threatened rule of absolute despotism, which Charlemagne's great successes had caused to be feared, the original establishment of the feudal system must be considered to have been a blessing to the European people. "Equally apart," says the great German historian, Friedrich von Raumer, "from the miserable servitude of oriental peoples, and from the cold obedience which many superficial minds consider only a necessary evil and which they reluctantly pay to their government, we see in it a personal attachment and reverence of the vassal for his lord and king, strengthened by the power derived from actual possession." Montesquieu also, one of the most enlightened writers on law, pays a sincere tribute to the original feudal organization when he says: "I do not believe that there has ever been established on the earth so well tempered a government; and it is to be admired how the corruption of the government of a conquering people formed the best sort of government which men were able to imagine." Von Raumer, again in comparing the three forms of government, uses this remarkable image: "An even plain and a solitary pillar erected upon it is the symbol of many unrestricted monarchies. All republics may be likened to a globe: each part of the animated surface seems equally important and worthy, and from seemingly opposite effects and counter-effects there yet arises one main tendency and movement. The symbol of feudality is a pyramid. From the base to the apex all parts are unchangeably united, down below the greatest number, and gradually decreasing, the king on the top. The pillar may fall down, or by military tyranny beat down the people; the globe may perchance roll beyond its assigned path, but nothing is more firmly grounded and in more safe equilibrium than the pyramid."

The history of the feudal age has itself curiously illustrated the image. Neither part of the pyramid was satisfied with its position. The top was powerless, and could communicate with the lower part, the people, only through the medium of the central part, or the nobles, and thus strove to remove that centre as much as possible, succeeding notably in France through the efforts of Cardinal Richelieu and Louis XIV., when they broke the power of the nobles. The central part thought it useless to support the upper part, of which it stood in no need, and strove to remove it as much as possible, succeeding in England by making a mere figure-head of the king, and in Germany by establishing itself into numberless small principalities. The lower part, the most numerous of all, meanwhile groaned and suffered all the time, until finally, in the earthquake of the French Revolution, it lifted up and overthrew at one and the same time king and nobles, proclaiming to an astonished world the sovereignty of the base, of the people.

Thus was doomed the pyramid; and the globe only remains as indeed the only stable and perfect figure for all government of man as for all nature, the figure in which the suns and stars move in eternal order and progress through endless space.

It was the inequality which the various parts of the pyramid bore to each other that proved its ruin: the prerogative of the higher, the nobles, and of the highest, the king, that weighed down too heavily upon the common people at the base.

During all these times of transition from feudal forms to monarchical and aristocratic institutions, only one great effort was made to establish a complete code of law for any people. This was done by Frederick II., emperor of the holy Roman empire (died 1250), one of the wisest and greatest men of his times, whose code of legislation for boldness and originality of conception, as well as for its comprehensiveness, has its counterpart only in the Institutes of Justinian and the Code of Napoleon. But far ahead of his age, and in constant combat with both the hierarchical despotism that then had grown up in Rome and extended itself over all Europe, and the money despotism that had just risen to a power never before displayed, permanent results could not follow his exertions, and with the downfall of the Hohenstaufen dynasty, arbitrary rule again usurped the place of law and justice in Europe.

Every sentiment of freedom on the part of the people died out; here and there only a small community establishing itself under a republican form of government, chiefly in cities like those of Northern Italy, and later the free cities of the North; until the cantons of Switzerland organized the first attempt of modern times to establish a rational federative republic. The Netherlands followed in the same direction, and in England also attempts have continually been made to establish its political state-organization upon republican principles of government.

For a time there was some hope that one of the great nations of Europe—the French—would emerge from this political chaos by establishing a form of government founded upon reason alone. The most awful convulsion of history overthrew for a time every prerogative that had been established, priestly, lordly, and kingly, and reasserted the right of every citizen of the state to equality under the law. But in the violence of the revolution the movement overleaped itself, and by establishing the prerogative of Paris, as the centralized ruler of France, created another despotism, whereby the promise of the beginning was killed off ere it was able to do more than fill Europe with a new feeling of freedom and exuberance, the like of which is not to be met with in all history, and which burns still, though under the ashes that were heaped upon it to suppress it. Even now it still animates the deeds of Gambetta, and perhaps with more hope of success those of the great tribune of Spain, Emilio Castelar.

Still, there is another result to be mentioned in this connection as indirectly proceeding from the French Revolution: the establishment of the Code Napoleon, which, taken all in all, is the most admirable and comprehensive system of laws yet produced by the mind of man.

For a time there was also hope that Germany would emerge from the rule of despotisms, and rise to political freedom in the same degree as it had always successfully vindicated for itself intellectual liberty. The revolutionary movement of 1848 began brightly enough, and, indeed, was at one time on the eve of success; but that same deplorable lack of unity and that same local state pride which put so many hindrances in the way of establishing our own Union, defeated the German when in its fullest glory. Since then the political history of Germany has been one of continual retrogression, so that now, through the unhappy conflict between France and Germany, it is enslaved even worse than it has been for centuries, under imperial rule, the extinction of all local self-government under the supreme law of the Prussian code, and the terrible conscription-system of the landwehr organization, which drives the despairing people by hundreds of thousands annually to seek refuge from tyranny by abandoning their native land.

It is one of the sarcasms of the spirit of history, that the victory of the Germans in the Franco-Prussian war should have resulted in Germanizing

France as it were, making her people sober, frugal, and industrious, and in Frenchifying Germany by deluging the nation with stock-monopolies and gambling-manias, such as effected the Vienna crisis, with French dissoluteness in its most extravagant forms, and latest of all with hierarchical alliances.

CHAPTER V.

SWITZERLAND AND GREAT BRITAIN.

Of all countries in Europe, it is only in Switzerland that the attempt to establish a rational form of federative government has been thus far crowned with success; although the introduction of the Referendum, whereby the laws, after their enactment by the legislative council of the Swiss Confederation, are submitted to the approval of the people, has of late greatly shaken the confidence of statesmen in the perpetuity of its institutions. Besides, the constitution of the Confederation is defective, in not providing a sufficient bond of union between the cantons, and they are mainly dependent upon foreign countries and bankers for their monetary means of intercommunication and commercial and business exchanges.

A most oppressive aristocracy of landed proprietors has also become established, which may eventually destroy the liberties of the people, by absorbing nearly all the political powers and official positions in the different cantons. This predominance of a landed aristocracy, the keystone of the feudal system, gives great permanence to the Swiss Confederation; but the result is the same there as elsewhere, to impoverish the masses of the people and eventually force them into the most abject labor slavery, as in England, China, Japan, Russia, and other countries where the same sort of aristocracy prevails.

In Great Britain, the representation of property, the integrity of the judiciary, and the universality of the laws for the encouragement of commerce and manufactures, have certainly thus far produced commercial, trading, and manufacturing prosperity, but only at the fearful cost of literally enslaving labor and impoverishing the masses. Still, the landed aristocracy of Great Britain, created by the feudal system, and holding the principal landed estates in the kingdom, has not been able to absorb the common liberties of the British subject to such an extent as to destroy them altogether, because the new sources of profitable employment opened up to the industrious middle classes in new colonies, the new powers applied to mechanics, and the new fields of wealth in gold, silver, commerce, banking, and exchanges, have raised many members of the poorer and middle classes to almost an equality in wealth with the richest peers of the realm.

On the other hand, while the Established Church has encountered too many opposing sects to become a very dangerous hierarchical element, save so far as it is united with the state, the royal charters, the money despotisms, the East India and other powerful companies and monopolies existing in the British empire, have always been held in check more or less by the hereditary aristocracy of the House of Lords, which overshadows and balances all the others. But the multitudinous complications of the British administration of public affairs, with its false systems of law, of government, of religious establishments, of education, and of the management of the colonies, cannot reasonably continue for any considerable period of time longer, and a revolution is now threatening, which will in all probability result in the peaceable establishment of a republican federative government over the United Kingdom and all its colonies. This would at once place the new republic of Great Britain in the front rank with the most powerful nations of the world, and relieve her people from the intolerable burdens of the feudal system, and all the aristocracies and monopolies that have followed in its train.

It has been well said that a revolution in Great Britain would not be a French revolution, accompanied by scenes of bloodshed, devastation, and carnage, but one moving in a quiet way for the creation of constitutional safeguards and just representative systems, to secure political equality under wise and harmonious codes to be established by the people in solemn conventions.

It will be the best for all the subjects of that country to unite in this grand movement for the common good, for if the aristocracies of monopolies or of birth force on a conflict between the people and themselves, the issue cannot be doubtful, and the losses will fall necessarily upon the parties now in possession of all that is valuable in the kingdom, and their utter ruin will be inevitable. For men are but men everywhere, with similar gifts, endowments, and passions. The hungry English laborer and the hungry French laborer have the same cravings for bread, for freedom, for equal political rights, and will not hesitate to use the same means to satisfy that craving. In truth, history would rather teach us that the Englishman is quicker to assert his rights, and more determined in removing every obstacle in the way of their assertion, than the Frenchman. The Magna Charta was extorted from King John by the English barons, while the kings of France were preparing for the subjection of their nobles, which Louis XIII. and Louis XIV. consummated. King Charles I. was beheaded long before the French followed the English example. While the descendants of the Norman conquerors, who appropriated nearly all the best lands of England, are still in possession of their vast estates, in France the lands of the nobles were divided among the people in the great revolution of 1789; and it is not improbable that the people of England, if forced into a revolutionary conflict with the ruling aristocracies, will naturally employ the same revolutionary measures to have those vast estates divided among the descendants of the former owners, which the French people found themselves compelled to employ.

No society can long keep its equilibrium that has at the one end such colossal wealth as, for instance, that of the Marquis of Westminster, with his annual income of more than a million of dollars, and at the other end full a million of penal paupers, several millions more of all kinds of laborers just on the verge of pauperism, and all of them suffering from impurity and ignorance; that hoards in the very centre of its civilization thousands upon thousands of men as fierce and lawless as the Goths and Huns that overran Europe under Attila, or the Tartars of Tamerlane, or the wretches of Faubourg St. Antoine, while it lavishes the money that should be spent at home upon their physical and intellectual improvement in Indian, Crimean, and Abyssinian wars, in enormous salaries of useless kings and queens, and extravagant dowers expended with the same profusion on all their children and relatives; that, forced on the one hand to make franchise more and more universal in the House of Commons, still retains, on the other hand, the only hereditary chamber in Europe, the House of Peers, a titled plutocracy, holding its vast entailed estates free of all military or civil duties, enjoying all the benefits of the feudal system without performing any of its duties, and whose only purpose of existence seems to be to veto every reform proposed by the representatives of the people in the House of Commons.

CHAPTER VI.

THE UNITED STATES.

I.

In the political organization of our own country, the most prominent and singular feature that presents itself is the fact, that our political constitution, our form of government, was an absolute creation of reason; not an hereditary accumulated set of laws or rules of political administration, but a specifically new political code; not the lawless growth of ages, but a rationally considered and determined form of government, made to fit a certain contingency. The code of Moses is, in this respect, the only one that has a similar origin; the legislation of the Hebrews did not arise gradually out of circumstances, like that of other nations, but was fixed complete at once to suit the miserable degraded condition of Hebrew slaves in Egypt.

Philosophers of great repute have denied the possibility of such an origin for a political constitution. Looking merely at the utterly irrational organization of the European monarchies,—the whole structure of which has reference only to the supreme welfare and monopoly of the ruling family,—and accepting these sad memorials of human cowardice and ignorance as glorious monuments of human power and wisdom, they have denied the possibility of any other origin of political organization, and laughed to scorn the attempt of the French revolutionists to erect a political fabric on principles of reason.

And yet here stands history with the purely rationally conceived government of Moses, of singular power and duration if its small territorial dimensions are taken into consideration, and the United States with nearly a century of history, more marvelous in its splendor and progress, despite all drawbacks, than the history of any other political organization in the world.

It is to be held one of the greatest blessings that the founders of our republic were thus enabled, under the peculiar exigencies of the case, to erect a new government of a federative republic altogether on principles of reason; and the only thing to be regretted is, that they did not carry out this principle in full by making rational organizations for the several separate States, by abolishing all laws for the perpetuation of slavery, by fixing the laws of money and commerce independently of traditional notions, and by establishing a complete code of laws—even as Napoleon established his Code for France—without the phantom of an unknown common law, which it is absurd to presume that the people should be able to follow, since the most distinguished judges of the different courts, State and federal, have been and still are continually announcing contradictory decisions, upon the same questions of law and equity, which are commonly known in law as vexed questions.

So far, therefore, as those great men followed purely the dictates of reason, their labors have been successful beyond precedent. So far as they followed the vagaries of tradition, on the other hand, they left the door open to the growth of moneyed monopolies and other forms of despotism that are showing their corrupting influence more and more every day, as well in absurd legislation as in the growth of ignorance and physical disease. It is easy to see how it chanced that they thus neglected to carry out the supreme rule of their political conduct in the details of law administration. Our form of government being a double one, the more extensive federal form naturally attracted their chief attention, and the separate State organizations with their exclusive management of "domestic affairs," engaged but to a local and limited extent the consideration of statesmen; and the anomaly of uniting these States under a purely rational form of government, while allowing them to retain all their historical and traditional legislation, escaped notice. These traditional features, it must be remembered, had been engrafted upon the several States that entered the Union while they were under monarchical rule, and thus their legislation partook—in some more and in some less—of the English feudal character. They became members of the Union with these feudal features and these English monarchical laws, with the barbarism of an unknown common law, of colonial slavery and other elements of prerogative power, judicial despotism, and money-monopoly worship, that still taint their political system, and which they in their turn engrafted more or less upon the new States that organized subsequently under the Union. All these feudal chains were incompatible with the idea of the new republic. It is amazing that this should have excited no attention or discussion, and that the people should have voluntarily saddled themselves with that huge body of legal despotism, the common law of England, of the true nature of which they were necessarily utterly ignorant. And yet they continued to put these shackles on their own young limbs, as one after another new States, with their constitutions, laws, municipal charters and ordinances, county and township regulations, organized themselves upon the old colonial foundations instead of the foundations of their own new federative republic.

Hence have naturally arisen constant conflicts and collisions between municipal and State laws, colonial laws and new State constitutions, State laws and federal laws, and federal laws and the United States Constitution; conflicts that have been a permanent source of uncertainty to the citizens, as to the nature and extent of their rights, and to their local officials, as to the extent of the powers conferred upon them. Hence all kinds of usurpations and monopolies have grown up, as a natural result of the want of proper checks and balances and well-adjusted State constitutions.

II.

It is evident that unless our form of government is to result in a failure, this state of things must be remedied by the application of principles founded upon universal truths. We must invent and determine for our separate State organizations organic laws that shall not interfere with the general form of our government and yet meet all the demands of a well-regulated State; that shall not merely afford security to persons and to property against direct violence and fraud, but protect men also from illegal monopolies, from fraud, impurity, and ignorance; that shall not merely in negative apathy permit the individual reformers and laborers in the fields of science and knowledge to prosecute their investigations, experiments, and researches, but shall extend to them proper aid, whereby all their labors may be joined in one common effort for the advancement of mankind, under a true and proper form of representative government. The unexpectedly rapid development of our States and the sudden growth of cities press with resistless force for the establishment of such a perfected system of State governments adapted to its own support. This is what the labor organizations mean when they clamor for changes which shall secure to them healthier dwelling-places and more time for self-culture; this is what outraged communities mean when they protest against the corrupt monopolies of the age, and the overshadowing despotism of railroad corporations that have neither local nor political connection with them, and yet place themselves beyond all regulations of order, safety, and economy from the communities their roads or their other monopolies have become a necessity to; and herein also lies the solution of the dangers threatened by the increase of the ignorant classes, which always accompanies the increase of monopolies and aristocracies.

At the same time we must amend our federal organization in such a way that it shall at once allow the separate States to make these additional laws, and itself assist in enforcing them. Thus, it is necessary for a true system of federative government to protect all citizens in their common rights of intercommunication by land, seas, oceans, rivers, and all highways. The railways, roadways, telegraphic lines, and all other channels of intercommunication and commerce, must be, in a federative republic, under the direction and control of the supreme or State governments. The people, who are the true source of all political and other power in a republic, control the state, and if the state controls the intercommunication between its citizens, the great franchises of free trade and commerce and of national money-making for national circulation will be preserved to the people, and not granted away to usurping monopolies, which thereby acquire by legislative grants the power to tax the people without their consent, in direct violation of the federal Constitution.

III.

I purpose now to trace out the fundamental principles and chief requirements of these our State organic laws, to show the necessity of a radical change, and detail the duties of a political commonwealth in making provision for the utmost development of the physical, intellectual, and moral faculties of its citizens; all the time, however, observing the limits within which such provisions may be made without trenching upon the rights of the individual for whose benefit alone each State and our federation was organized. It is in this latter point that my work will find its relation to the commentaries of our great constitutional expounders, as well as its distinction from the arbitrary dogmas of writers like Plato, Rousseau, Voltaire, and others, who may have had invention enough to propound gilded theories of an ethical government, but lacked legal training to determine its limits by the universal conception of law as applied to the government of a State designed to belong to a federation of several States.

IV.

In part, even our present forms of State legislation transcend the limited sphere of mere direct protection against violence and fraud. Nor can it well be otherwise, so soon as people come in close contact with each other. So long as men live at considerable distances from each other, on tracts of land large enough to prevent the immediate perception of injurious influences upon each other by improper construction of their dwellings, for instance, or uncleanliness and disease of their bodies, and so long as commerce and money have not yet collected into great centres, and thus established despotic monopolies, legislation for protection against such injurious influences and monopolies will not even be thought of. Such was the general condition of the people of the United States in former times; and when gradually larger cities began to grow up, and railways, banks, and commerce to assume gigantic proportions, it did not at first occur to their inhabitants that another class of laws had become necessary than the class which had been sufficient to secure life, liberty, and property from direct assault and tyrannic oppression. It was only constant and continued experience, pressing for the inauguration of measures that were found necessary, which dictated a legislation that was rather merely submitted to than accepted, from a comprehension of its necessity and justice. In this way municipal ordinances regulating the building of houses, the behavior of persons, the power of corporations, and a thousand other matters that had been considered the exclusive concern of individual notion and inclination, were tacitly acquiesced in, and taxes for sanitary, reformatory, and other purposes paid without very earnest opposition. Nevertheless, the doubt of their legality always remained; nor was the general principle of these measures ever laid down and determined. It seems strange indeed, and yet it is none the less true, that there really was not and is not any difference in the general principle of legality underlying these measures, and that the only doubt and difficulty respecting them arose and arises from the consideration of the necessary space to be allowed for the inhabitants of cities and villages. It is the distance, the extent of space between one farm and another, which in their cases renders it difficult to perceive that there is an actual injury done by one man to another, an infringement perpetrated upon the individual's right to life, liberty, and property. We can see easily the direct connection between the injury and the deed when one man kills or assaults another in the street, but it is rather a difficult matter to trace injurious effects to the neighbor who builds a vitriol or a gas factory near my house, or builds an adjoining dwelling with insufficient drainage, etc.; and, nevertheless, the encroachment upon my life, or it may be upon my property, is the same in either case.

V.

Should such amendments to the organic laws of the States of the federation as I purpose here to sketch be adopted, results would follow surpassing even the dreams our most sanguine political patriots have dared to indulge in. A body of men and women would be raised, healthy, and intellectually cultivated, to a degree which would make them as nearly as possible inaccessible to physical and moral evils, fit exponents and representatives of the ideal that gave life to them.

The world of nature it would change and turn into a grand landscape-garden, æsthetically representative of the world of mind and freedom, under equal laws, the fit habitation of such noble beings as men can become, a true kingdom of God on earth, every element of nature subject to the free and harmonious directing powers of the human mind. Far from disfiguring or making ungainly the aspect of nature, as they do now, men's habitations, the cities, houses, streets, alleys, boulevards, etc., would fall into harmony with their natural sites, and by architectural beauty, order, and cleanliness irradiate loveliness in every direction.

It would make all men equal under just laws by regulating their intercommunication through money and commerce in a rational manner, by raising up the lowest to the highest degree of culture, and securing to each individual through an organized system of labor sufficient leisure to acquire the greatest freedom and knowledge. The existing rivalry between rich and poor would thus cease of itself and find its amelioration, if not its annihilation, in a common co-operative effort to realize the highest good and happiness for all.

In its ultimate results it would dispel from the minds of men every element of darkness and superstition. For in the highest school of the State, the university, the highest science, the philosophy of knowledge, would be taught, and would illuminate every region of human knowledge by analyzing that knowledge itself. The foolish fear of an angry God would change into adoration of his love and wisdom, and the superstitious dread of the future world into serene and happy assuredness of infinitely continuing revelations of new beauty. Men would no longer harass their minds and souls with idle speculation, but would work out their true mission, to attain the greatest good, happiness, and wisdom. For to enable men to do this should be the exclusive final end and aim of a government of law.

Even as the grand aim of the divine government of the universe is manifestly by wise, harmonious, and progressive laws of development to work out to fullest perfection all forms, faculties, and intelligences of the creatures on our earth, so a human government of law should resemble as nearly as may be this divine government of nature, and should, therefore, in its organic constitutional code, provide for the attainment of the greatest good, happiness, and wisdom by the people of the state; and as the permanence and certainty of the laws of nature are necessary for the preservation of the divine order of nature and the lives of all the creatures existing in it, so the certainty and permanence of the organic laws of a state are necessary for the preservation of human order, or true freedom under the law, so that all persons in the state may attain and enjoy the greatest good and happiness of which their organization and faculties are capable, without in any way interfering with the proper freedom, activity, and happiness of others.

CHAPTER VII.

FUNDAMENTAL PRINCIPLES.

THE fundamental principle of such a constitutional code is:

AFFIRMATIVELY: To provide for the harmonious, temperate, fit, and best use attainable of all the faculties of mind and body of each person, so that each one may have, under the law, the possibility of attaining, without any of the hindrances of ignorance, impurity, fraud, or tyranny, the greatest good, happiness, wisdom, beauty, love, and perfection of which his faculties and organization are capable: 1st, for himself; 2d, for his family; 3d, for the society or state in which he lives.

NEGATIVELY: To prohibit each person from intemperate, inharmonious, reckless, hurtful, or unfit abuse or use of either or any of the faculties of his mind and body.

These two propositions will validate and test the true objects of all codes, constitutions, and laws, and the true character of all legislative, judicial, and executive, governmental operations, for the government of men under State and federative systems of representative governments.

CHAPTER VIII.

ANALYSIS OF FUNDAMENTAL PRINCIPLES.

THE essence of man is freedom. It is this that distinguishes him from all other beings, and makes it impossible to mistake him for a mere animal. All other beings are complete in bodily organization; man alone is incomplete. All other bodies are sufficient and perfectly determined in their structure; but the body of man is insufficient, and simply infinitely determinable. What he is at birth we know not; what he is to be is to be wrought out in him by his own freedom and activity, under just and comprehensive laws.

It is by token of this freedom, when manifested in the world of nature, that man proclaims his presence over the gulf of many thousand years, and in the rudest tools or arms of prehistoric times announces his existence. History is nothing but a record of man's strife for the attainment of this freedom in its highest degree externally, through forms of government; culture nothing but an endeavor to realize it internally. And since neither development can be achieved separately, the establishment of a state organization, which shall enable man to secure the fullest freedom of mind, of person, and of activity, must necessarily accompany and be accompanied by higher culture and progress. It is only in a properly constructed state organization that man can attain that complete self-determination, that development and subjection to his free control of all the faculties of his mind and body, whereby he will be enabled to use them fitly and harmoniously, under judicious and wise laws, for the realization of the greatest good and happiness life is to give and express, and to constitute himself a truly rational being.

No one individual in a state can be secure in his freedom under the laws, unless every other individual is prohibited from interfering with it. Had each individual attained full development of his moral nature and freedom, this prohibitory character of law would be unnecessary, for the free wills of all would of themselves harmonize in the idea of the greatest good. But as this full development does not exist, and is rather the very object to be realized, the inharmonious and unfit use of the mental and bodily faculties of the one individual constantly interferes with the freedom and progress of the others, and thus needs the prohibition of its inharmonious exercise. Men in establishing governments of law must adopt the plan manifested in those laws that are established upon fixed principles of universal application, and announce themselves in unvarying succession.

Upon these two fundamental principles, affirmative and negative, all laws and governments of law are grounded; through them alone the achievement of an ultimate ethical and legal organization within the state made possible. Another six thousand years might pass away, and bring mankind but little nearer to its ideal, unless these principles were carried out in a state organization, and eventually established over the whole extent of a federative republic. Great moral and intellectual advancement of the race is but a dream so long as there are wretched, ignorant, and wicked on all sides in a state to check and injure the development of higher culture; so long as filth, folly, and impropriety everywhere offend the purer, wiser, and more cultured persons, there can be but limited and obstructed advancement; and legislation has hitherto looked upon these matters as if it had no concern with them at all. Thus the highest of all arts and the grandest of all sciences, the art and science of statesmanship, in the noblest sense of the word, the art and science of organizing men into a complete harmonious union and activity, wherein each one shall have all his faculties developed to their highest practical possibility, and wherein all shall artistically and scientifically combine to make their common property, the earth, a beautiful and harmoniously cultivated whole, a paradise, not of primitive nature and idleness, but of cultivated reason, scientific knowledge, and joyful labor, has hitherto not even been possible, for want of a state organization wherein to establish and apply it.

In no other way than by means of such a state and federative organization can the citizens achieve their true destination as freemen, worthy to enjoy "liberty and law" under federative government. In no other way can the gigantic conflict between men and nature be successfully carried on to victory, their forces and knowledge being severally cultivated to their highest perfection, and assigned to specific parts of an organized plan.

It is only by means of a practical code of self-supporting laws, providing for the purity, health, training, education, protection, political equality, and happiness of each citizen, and regulating under general laws all intercommunication between all persons, that the people can be fully protected from the selfishness, tyranny, extortion, ambition, wickedness, and crimes of the many monopolizing, fraudulent, and corrupt organizations—many of them springing up from the late war between the States—always vigilantly watching every opportunity to rob the masses of their rights, franchises, and liberties, for the benefit of the few despots who rapaciously swallow up the resources of the States and the nation, by using the government itself as the chief instrument of their tyranny, by bribing and corrupting the traitorous agents of the people—the State and federal legislatures—to grant to their monopolies the public lands, the public charters, the common public rights of intercommunication, of banking, of telegraphing, and of using the public highways and the public domain with electro-magnetic telegraphs and with steam railways.

The individual alone may, to some extent, realize his destination and ideal in his own internal cūlture; but as a member of humanity, and citizen of a state, he cannot achieve even this, his own end, perfectly, unless he assists in achieving the destination of his kind by co-operation and united effort under wise and just laws, and in keeping down all forms of despotism in his state. The subjugation of nature, and all her turbulent elements, is a task utterly beyond the power of individuals, and until their subjugation is completed no individual can rise to his own highest development.

To attain these ends the constitutional codes will have to apply the above fundamental principles to the three functions of man, as—1st, a physical body in the world of nature; 2d, an intelligent being in the world of intelligence; and 3d, a social being in the world of the state; and hence it will have to legislate in its positive character concerning—

1. Public hygiene.
2. Public education.
3. Public intercommunication.

And in its negative character concerning the—

1. Establishment of a constitutional code.
2. Establishment of a code of laws.
3. Establishment of a federative and an international code, to secure liberty and law against all the powers of despotism.

I. PUBLIC HYGIENE.

CHAPTER I.

PURE AIR.

THE human body, being the material representative of the human mind, should like it irradiate health and cleanliness, and in proportion as it does not do so it contributes to moral disease and impurity. There is no more effective propagator of immorality than the filth of crowded districts in cities; it infects the body with all the physical diseases that stir up vicious and low appetites and passions. The law should protect every citizen against these injurious influences, and as they operate chiefly through the air, it is the duty of a state organization to secure to every citizen the needful amount of pure air wherever the co-residence of others tends to impair its natural purity.

Pure air is, indeed, the foremost necessity of human life. Not only does man need it as food,—and as food he consumes in quantity six thousand times more of air than of all other food,—but also to preserve the normal temperature of the body, and carry off its exhalations. It is only of late years that the facts connected with the consumption of air by the human body have been mathematically ascertained, and corroborated by experiments, particularly by Dr. von Pettenkofer, the most eminent sanitary physician of Germany, as, indeed, the whole science of public hygiene is but a few years old. The results ascertained disclose enormous figures. Whereas but thirty years ago, for instance, six hundred cubic feet of fresh air per hour were considered sufficient for each patient in a hospital, over two thousand cubic feet per hour have been ascertained to be necessary; an amount which, in such large buildings as hospitals necessarily are, and still more in crowded cities, only the most efficient system of artificial mechanical ventilation can secure. Not to provide for this constant flow of pure air throughout every house, street, and alley, is to spread disease in every form from one body to another, and, moreover, to steep the whole population of a city into a continuous intoxication, the result of inhaling the poisonous carbonic acid gas infecting the air.

Every species of intoxication imparts a fondness for the condition, a desire to recur to the sensations excited by it; and the intoxication produced by foul air is not without this dangerous element, which, indeed, alone could have made it possible that men should shut out from their dwelling-places God's pure air as if it were their worst enemy, and yield themselves and their children to those sensations of drowsiness and stupor which air impregnated with carbonic acid gas invariably excites. Legislation on this subject will, therefore, meet a deep-rooted opposition from the frequenters of dens, cellars, etc.; but in proportion as this opposition has its origin in that same foul air, the law should protect the up-growing generation from similar results, and make possible the raising of a new generation of children whose bodies shall be free from the fearful taint. The terrible epidemics from which the human race suffers periodically have their chief carrier and nourisher in foul air, even as the unproportionally enormous mortality of infants must be ascribed chiefly to the poisonous atmosphere of nurse-rooms, from which the pure air for which the infants cry is shut out even with greater care than from the other rooms of the house. That foul air is the chief agent in spreading contagion and epidemics has been now demonstrated beyond a doubt, and the fact which has so often excited wonder, that epidemics seem to gather additional intensity in winter-time, is a striking proof of it. The wonder was excited by a notion that the cold air of winter must be purer than the warmer air of summer, and produce of itself better ventilation in a house. But the reverse is the case. Unless a room has a good fire in an open chimney in winter-time the ventilation is much less than in summer-time, when windows and doors are thrown open, and hence in winter the air is more impure in unheated rooms. Now the miserable dwellings of the poor are but too often without fire; at night-time, particularly, few of them can afford to keep up a fire. Thus the dread agent of contagion and pestilence gains additional strength from misery and poverty;

and it is for this reason that fuel should be provided for the poor in winter-time, as one of the most effective means to ventilate their wretched dwellings, as they now exist under our present defective system of house-building, even in cities containing crowded populations.

To provide pure air for every person, and thus protect each from the contaminating influences of all kinds of miasmatic and other impurities, the legislative power in each state must regulate:

1. The laying out of cities and villages in such a manner as to make possible the needful ventilation of their buildings, and providing public drainage.

2. The construction of all private as well as public buildings in such a manner as to make accessible to every inmate the necessary quantity of pure air, and the establishing of private drainage.

3. Personal cleanliness.

4. The laying out of counties and townships.

To provide, furthermore, all other kinds of food and drink for the human body in their natural condition of healthful purity, the legislative power in each state must regulate:

1. The sale of all food and drinks consumed by man, so as to secure them to the consumer in their unadulterated purity.

2. The preservation of the health of all animals, birds, and fishes, and the soundness of all vegetables consumed by man.

CHAPTER II.

LAYING OUT OF CITIES.

THE laying out of cities according to principles of sanitary science is practicable only, of course, in new cities, or in new additions to cities already existing, though it may in many cases be possible also to rebuild old and badly built cities on a sanitary plan; at least in part, as Paris, for instance, was remodeled, and as large fires and other circumstances make such reforms practicable in all cities.

In this matter it is first of all necessary that the state should determine and establish for all cities and villages the minimum width of boulevards, streets, and alleys, and the proportionate number of open public squares. In my judgment every fourth street should be a boulevard, and every fourth square in every direction would constitute the proper proportion for public squares. At least a part of these squares, and the centre and side lines of the boulevards also, should be planted with trees, to absorb the carbonic acid gas with which the air of a crowded city is always surcharged, and furnish shade for the inhabitants. With such squares and wide boulevards and streets, sufficient pure air can be made accessible to even the most central parts of a large city, to meet the requirements of every building and of every human being, and of every bird and animal therein. Arboreal vegetation also aids very much in the purification of the air, and the public squares could be made more useful by the planting of trees in them, the opening of fountains, and the erection of public baths in the centre, and furnishing pure, cool water for drinking.

It is further necessary that the state or the municipal corporation should provide for all cities and villages a perfect system of drainage. The ground below, as well as the air around and above us, requires continuous and thorough purification. Next to the air the soil is the main carrier of epidemical and other diseases, and being less susceptible than the atmosphere of continuous purification, it has been considered necessary by the most experienced sanitary officials to prohibit the habitation of all underground rooms, whether cellars or basements, and to insist upon an air-tight cementing of all the walls and floors of cellars and basements.

A perfect system of drainage for a city or village must determine the number, sites, and outlets of main sewers and the branch sewer-pipes to each house. All the sewers and sewer-pipes should be laid as deep as practicable under the ground, and should be built as air-tight as possible, since it has been abundantly demonstrated that the common sewers and cast-iron sewer-pipes, without close-fitting valves, allow the penetration of the vicious gases generated in them, which thus spread from below into the houses. All sewer-openings on the streets or alleys should have air-tight valves to admit the surface water, without allowing the escape of noxious vapors.

Arrangements should be made for the removal of the sewage and its chemical disinfection, so that it may be speedily returned to the soil to which it belongs, as its most potent fertilizer, and which in its turn is for it the most complete final disinfectant.

Both these requirements of a good sewer system are secured by the one now adopted and carried out in many parts of Great Britain, and should at once be made to replace our system, whereby the great rivers are generally made the receptacles of the filth of the sewers, the wretched effects whereof in London led to the adoption of the present system. So offensive had the smell from the Thames, and from the clogged-up sewers opening into the Thames, become, that a general clamor arose for the abolition of all sewers; and Faraday, in a letter to the London *Times* of 1854, was constrained to say: "The smell was very bad and common to the whole of the water; it was the same as that which now comes up from the gully-holes in the streets. The whole river was for a time a real sewer." It was then that the present system was proposed, by means of which the sewage of all parts of London is carried far away from the city to places where it can be utilized, by drainage so deep as practically to prevent the escape of its gases through the soil. Thus the same agency of drainage secures health to the city by taking from it that which is unwholesome to man, and bringing it to the soil, to which it restores health and strength.

Our own lands need every day more and more this invigorating sewage, and the cities along our great rivers need to be freed from the miasmatic influences they carry along as it is borne on by their waters.

Thus Professor Liebig writes: "Of all the elements of the fields which, in their products, in the shape of corn and meal, are carried into the cities and there consumed, nothing, or as good as nothing, returns to the fields. It is clear that if these elements were collected without loss, and every year restored to the fields, they would then retain the power to furnish to the cities the same quantity of corn and meal, and it is equally clear that if the fields do not receive back these elements agriculture must soon suffer. In regard to the utility of the avails of the sewage of towns as manures, no farmer, and scarcely any intelligent person, entertains a doubt."

Our modern facilities for transportation, and for removing all kinds of compost by mechanical appliances, should induce all municipal corporations to apply these powers to the desired object, so that the diurnal purification of each city and village should be as regular in its progress as the succession of day and night, and the vast amounts of filth of all kinds that now poison the water-courses, the fish, and the people living near river-banks, may be returned to the soil at many more or less distant points in the surrounding country.

For this purpose, moreover, the streets of every city should be regularly swept every night, and the dirt, together with the sewage, taken to the soil of the agriculturist for its rejuvenation. By thus keeping the streets clean, it will also be practicable to sprinkle them through the day, during the dusty season, and thereby to moisten the heated air to its normal condition, and refresh the exhausted bodies of the inhabitants. Every city should inaugurate such a system of sprinkling the streets.

The fire departments of every city, having a plentiful water supply, can very easily extend their functions so as to effect this cleaning and sprinkling of the streets. All the cities along rivers, for instance, can without much cost have their streets every day regularly washed from the water-plugs arranged for the fire-engines. As matters stand at present, people wait for a heavy rain to accomplish this. But heavy rains do not come at our bidding, and light ones only make the condition of streets worse. It behooves man to help himself, and not wait upon the irrational forces of nature, that may send down a heavy rain when it is a positive injury, and withhold the moisture when all the earth cries for it. We must learn to control this, and provide by art against the irregularity of the action of natural forces.

The soil being, next to the air, the most active agent in spreading disease and epidemic matter, it is evident that the soil-water of cities and villages, their springs and wells, must be generally of an unhealthy character, and unfit to be used for drinking purposes. Hence public water-works are very essential for the preservation of health, and their construction and use should be insisted on wherever this is at all practicable. But besides their great sanitary value, they are indispensable for the purposes of drainage, for watering the streets and parks, and all the vegetation of a city, and for the establishment of sufficient baths.

Gas-works, with their constant efflux of sulphureted hydrogen, should never be tolerated within the city limits, and in the laying of gas-pipes it should be seen to that they are put at as great a depth as practicable under the ground, and made tight and secure against the escape of gas. Indeed, all factories that emit foul odors and poison the air should be removed far from the city and disinfected daily.

Nor should slaughter-houses be tolerated within the city, and the strictest control should be exercised over them to secure the removal of all noxious matter and the disinfection of their offal. The public health of every city demands that a rational system of abattoirs should supersede the present miserably unsystematic arrangement of slaughter-houses, with their inevitably accompanying nuisances of soap, fat, etc.; establishments concerning which the New York Board of Health says: "It is positively asserted that more noxious gases escape into the air from this source than would result from the decomposition of human bodies if the whole island were a grave-yard." It makes one blush to reflect that these life-destroying establishments are still tolerated in the midst of large cities, when so far back as the reign of Henry VII. a petition was addressed to the king, from several parishes of the city of London, affirming that the said "parishes were greatly annoyed and distempered by corrupt air engendered in the said parishes by reason of the slaughter of beasts had and done in the butchery of St. Nicholas;" which petition called forth an enactment that "no butcher or his servant is to slay any beast within the walls of London, or any walled town in England, under a penalty," etc.

CHAPTER III.

CONSTRUCTION OF BUILDINGS.

A GENERAL building law should be passed for the erection of all new buildings, and another law requiring that all buildings already erected should have such practical changes and improvements as may be expedient to conform them to the rules of sanitary science.

For executing such a building law two classes of commissioners should be joined in a board to be appointed: architects and sanitary officers. The architectural commissioners will have to see that the necessary architectural requirements for buildings are complied with, as to thickness of walls, strength of foundations, fire-escapes, fireproof externally, etc.; the sanitary commissioner in conjunction with the architect must supervise the sanitary requirements, such as the height of the building itself, of its several stories, of its windows, and their position in regard to light and fresh air; the water-closets and their proper connection with the general sewer; the construction of the kitchen with reference to cleanliness, absorption or removal of all fumes, stenches, etc., and immediate removal of all offal and dirt; the proper supply of bath-rooms, and such a system of ventilation and disinfection as the exigencies of the building may require.

To cut off as much as possible communication between the house and the soil, the floors and walls of every cellar and basement should be made as air-tight as possible, and the habitation of cellars and basements should be absolutely forbidden.

The habitation of any new dwelling within three months after its erection, though it be purified by fire in each room and in the cellar, should be forbidden, as the enormous quantity of moisture which new walls, etc., contain, cannot evaporate before that time, and during its presence renders such dwellings dangerously unhealthy.

It having been clearly demonstrated that the natural ventilation of buildings by windows, chimneys, and other vents is altogether insufficient to meet the requirements of the human body, an artificial system must be prescribed, whereby the necessary quantity of pure air can be brought into every room of each house and the impure air constantly expelled. The revolving hot and cold air furnace accomplishes this object.

All buildings should be inspected semi-annually by the official architectural and sanitary commissioners, both in regard to their safety and their healthfulness, and the result published and reported; the report to specify all particulars, and to state the number of inmates, so that the overcrowding of houses and rooms, which makes proper ventilation impossible and spreads diseases and crimes in so many portions of our large cities, may be prohibited.

In the erection of high buildings in cities, with many large windows of plate or other glass, external shades above the window-tops should be provided, to prevent as far as practicable the radiation and reflection of the solar rays and avoid the increase of heat, that will add several degrees to the natural warmth of summer. It has been conjectured, perhaps without sufficient grounds, that an extensive refraction of the solar rays in midsummer might affect the regularity of the ebb and flow of the electro-magnetic tides, and increase the formation of carbonic acid gas in the air of a badly ventilated city; but whether these injurious effects arise from this cause or not, the fact that it increases the natural heat of the climate in summer, is injurious to the eyes, and induces sunstrokes, should arrest the attention of the legislator.

The almost total absence of smoke-consumers in the factories, distilleries, breweries, and furnaces used in cities, is another source of injury and annoyance to the inhabitants, causing the escape of large volumes of foul gases, and enveloping the place with soot and foul odors. The manufacturers using coal should be required to provide the common inventions for burning the carbonaceous particles that now escape from their furnace fires, and as much of the smoke as may be practicable, whereby they will economize fuel and promote the health and cleanliness of the citizens.

CHAPTER IV.

PERSONAL CLEANLINESS.

THE air cannot be kept pure and safe if impure bodies fill it constantly with foul exhalations. Impurity is as well the cause as the effect of disease and contagion. Hence personal uncleanliness is not merely an offense to the senses, but a bodily injury; and purity of body becomes an indispensable requisite in large cities, where the bodies of men constantly jostle against each other, and the exhalations therefrom are so extensive.

Nothing will tend so much to promote personal cleanliness as the provision of pure air. Purity of one kind will excite a desire for purity in all forms. Properly laid out cities and well-constructed houses may therefore be supposed of themselves to secure the necessary personal cleanliness. But the establishment of baths in every house and on every floor of a house, where they are built for the habitation of more than one family, as well as the baths to be constructed for public use in every fourth square of a city, will tend still further to secure this necessary requisite of physical and moral health, and make special legislation on the subject superfluous. On the other hand, pure air can be enjoyed only by those persons who preserve their own personal cleanliness, and secure the most thorough ventilation of their workshops, offices, and dwellings. Heat, light, and electricity can be enjoyed perfectly only by those who inhale pure air, which gives man heat and strength from the oxygen consumed through his lungs, renewing his animal heat and power every instant of his life. For air is truly the chief nourisher in life's feast, the elemental supply that enables man to move and execute the functions and faculties of mind and body. Hence the imperious duty of the State to provide for the preservation of the purity of the air at any cost, as the element of prime necessity, absolutely indispensable to the happiness, health, and life of its citizens every moment of their existence.

CHAPTER V.

LAYING OUT OF COUNTIES AND TOWNSHIPS.

EVEN the agricultural districts, where men live so far apart that the injurious influence of one body upon the other through the air is difficult of ascertainment, demand, under the guidance of modern sanitary science, some general laws whereby to secure each citizen of those districts immunity from harm, and the inhabitants of cities protection against the miasmatic poisons in the currents of air swept along from such districts by the winds.

Each county should above all have a complete system of drainage to purify and fertilize the soil, which in the extensive districts of the country is of the same relative importance as the purification of air is in the cities, and so arranged as to make the drain-water also useful in the drier parts of the district for purposes of irrigation.

Each county should next arrange a sufficient system of forest parks, or wooded lands, whereby to purify the air and water, and extend to their soil that protection which causes the tree-covered oasis to bloom forth in perennial beauty, furnishing water, vegetation, and shade to the weary traveler in the midst of the desolation of Sahara. For the influence of such parks, with their arboreal ventilation, extends not only to the health of the farmer, but also to the productiveness of the soil. Its sure and immediate operation in this respect has been very effectively illustrated on our Western plains, where by the judicious planting of trees vast districts have been reclaimed for agriculture that were formerly considered irredeemably unproductive. And as the waters of the Alps have brought under cultivation the once arid plains of Northern Italy, directed thither by skillful engineering, so might the heavy snows and rains that fall in the Sierra Madre, instead of being allowed to swell the floods of the Missouri, and of the other great rivers south of its source, and bring destruction to their rich bottom lands, be used to assist in irrigating the vast barren districts that extend from the mountains eastwardly. Combined with the influence of the trees now being planted on those plains, the waters from the Rocky Mountains, directed by science to effect irrigation, would cause them to bloom forth into a paradise of vegetation, as if by magic.

To obtain this necessary arboreal ventilation and protection for every part of the country, a park with trees of one hundred and sixty acres should be laid out in each section of six hundred and forty acres of land, and each road in the county should be laid out with a double row of trees, the whole supervision of which should be assigned to the agricultural schools of each county. The parks could be stocked with all kinds of singing and other birds that protect the trees, gardens, and fields against insects and vermin. The soil of the parks could also be sown with grass, and various kinds of grazing animals admitted to lend additional charms to the landscape.

If at all possible—and a judicious system of canals in every State would make such a contrivance quite practicable—each county should also be provided with a sufficient sheet of water, stocked with various productive and healthy fishes, to furnish food to the inhabitants and purify the water. These artificial or natural lakes would add materially to the health of the neighborhood by moistening the air and absorbing on its part the impurities of the atmosphere.

Such a system of parks, trees, and lakes would clothe the whole landscape with rare beauty, and cause it to breathe forth sweetness, fragrance, and health. Nor should the system be confined to the counties. Besides these county parks, it would be recommendable to set aside in the several States, wherever it is practicable, a more extensive tract of forest grounds, such as is now proposed for the State of New York in the Adirondacks, with their more than eight hundred thousand acres of a magnificent forest, that secures to the beautiful Hudson its perennial flow of waters, and sweetens every current of air that sweeps over it, and such as Congress has secured in the magnificent park of the Yosemite Valley, for the common recreation and enjoyment of the American people.

Congress should also grant lands for State parks, one or more in number, to the new States and to the Territories, for the use of the people of each State and Territory forever. Congress should also grant to the same States and Territories, for the use of the agricultural schools, three by three sections of land in one tract in each county for the establishment, use, and support of agricultural, mining, mechanical, and other schools, to be devoted to such purposes forever. There should also be reserved six sections of land in each township of thirty-six sections for the support of the other schools, colleges, and universities proposed to be established in this work, so that a permanent endowment may be created for public education for all time to come.

By such a system of parks, etc.—more especially if it is accompanied by the planting of odorous flowers in swampy localities; flowers that destroy by their exhalations of ozone all the impurities of the air—the malarious diseases now familiar to agricultural districts will be gradually subdued, a greater evenness of temperature gradually secured, and all nature placed under additional control and direction by the science and art of man.

These forest parks will break the violence of storms, inhale, as it were, the surcharge of electricity from the clouds and the impurities of the air, and while feeding on these exhalations and those of the water, restore to all forms of life the pure oxygen for vitality. By means of this arboreal and floral ventilation and purification of the air of rural districts, the inhabitants of all cities near them will be furnished with pure, invigorating air, while the aspect of all the fresh life of the trees, plants, and water will irradiate in every direction new sensations of pleasure, of enjoyment, and of health.

The comparatively new country composing our republic is still only sparsely populated, and amply large enough to furnish its present and future inhabitants, for many years to come, with room in all villages, cities, townships, and counties for the introduction of all sanitary safeguards herein proposed for the preservation of the purity of the air, the food and the drinks consumed by the people, and to furnish them the means for recreation, amusement, and physical development.

CHAPTER VI.

PURE FOOD AND DRINK.

In the primitive condition of man each individual furnished himself his own food and drink, and legislation to secure men from adulteration of the articles of diet was therefore unnecessary. But as men began to divide occupations and professions among each other, it became necessary that measures should be adopted to secure to the purchasers the purity of their food and drinks. The practice of adulterating the various articles used by men for consumption, has indeed been carried to such a point, and is productive of such disastrous results in the spread of disease and crime, that the most stringent legislation has become necessary.

In every community, therefore, a board of inspectors, composed of men sufficiently educated in the necessary chemical and other studies to qualify them for the office, should be appointed, and intrusted with full power to supervise all markets and other places where those articles are exposed for sale, to supervise all slaughter-houses, and examine into the healthy condition of all animals intended for consumption, and also into the processes of fattening and feeding the animals, so that all vicious methods of using distillery-swill, malt-mash, still-slop, and other deleterious diet may be abolished. They should also report the manner in which animals are brought to market, and see that they do not become diseased by being crowded into unventilated cars, or by being driven beyond their strength, or by cruel treatment, or deprivation of food and drink on the way. Few persons have any notion of the enormous proportion of diseased meat brought to market under the present loose system, where the owner of the cattle conspires with the railroad people to crush as many sheep or cattle into a close car as the space will allow without suffocation.

These commissioners should also prepare game-laws, and laws regulating the introduction of productive and healthy fish into the different rivers and lakes of the State.

They should also have power to inspect all liquors, wines, milk, alcoholic and other drinks, consumed by the people, before they are offered for sale, at such times as may be deemed necessary, to prevent the poisoning or adulteration of drinks; and likewise to inspect all drugs and medicines, so that none but pure articles may be put up for sale.

They should also provide pure vaccine matter in proper quantities; examine wells and water-works, and report on the condition of the water, after submitting it to all usual tests.

It may appear to many at the first glance rather too critical that I should enter into these minute details of sanitary regulations in a book on law and government. Let any one go to the Five Points, or along Baxter Street, of New York, and scent the vicious gases that arise from every house and alley, filling the streets with most poisonous odors and exhalations, and he may realize how utterly futile must be every effort to reclaim the human race and lift up those human wrecks from their debasing condition, unless such measures as I have proposed are adopted and carried out in their minutest details. Let him enter their terrible tenement-houses, and note the haggard faces, drooping bodies, and eyes that glisten with vice in proportion as they have drawn in the reflection of vice and impurity on every side in these miserable rooms! Let him go next into the wealthier parts of the city, and smell through every water-pipe of the closet, the bath-room, and the washstand the same diseased smells of Five Points and Baxter Street, breathe in every breath of air the same foul, curse-laden atmosphere, and he may realize the claim of one human being to be protected against the poisonous exhalations of another! Or let him enter our street-cars, our coaches, our railroad-cars, with their closed windows shutting out the pure air of God and forcing rank poison down his lungs!

The new civilization cannot come or show itself except through healthy bodies ruled by healthy minds; and we cannot get health except through purity. Purity of air, of food, and of drinks will give us that physical health which, both strengthened by and supporting mental and moral purity, can alone raise our race to the high perfection which lies within its reach. The impurity of food and air has so accustomed men to impurities of all kinds that chastity has almost become a reproach, and men plunge into vice as naturally as into a foul-scenting atmosphere, or as they eat the diseased meats and the decayed vegetables sold in the market-places.

It is to remedy this state of things in its first and most immediate appearance that the inauguration of such a sanitary system as I have described becomes the first duty of the law-maker. I well know that of recent years steps have been taken to secure this object. Nay, even a national public health association has been organized to effect some of the measures herein proposed. But all these efforts have been merely sporadic and partial; and even in Germany, where, during the past few years, the science of public hygiene has at last been recognized as entering into one of the most needful departments of state government, and been cultivated to an extent beyond that of any other country, a thorough and sweeping reformation has not been effected.

An amateur national health society is not what we need, but a sanitary department in each State government especially for this branch of the public service, which should collect all the statistics that are still wanting in relation to the laws governing the dissemination of diseases and epidemics, and the hygienic and sanitary measures whereby their propagation can be arrested, showing also the influence of all the various kinds of food and drinks, occupations, recreations, and habits of life upon the happiness, civilization, and health of the people, with ample powers to enforce all the regulations necessary to carry out its beneficent objects.

Nor should it be forgotten that the sanitary measures recommended in this work would not only check disease and crime, eradicate hereditary ailments and infirmities, but they would beautify, adorn, and utilize nature everywhere. Let any one picture to himself a city such as I have described, with every fourth square a public park, with forest shade-trees, public baths, and fountains of pure water for drinking, every fourth street a grand, airy, clean, and shaded boulevard, having double rows of shade-trees on each side and in the centre, and all the other streets with single rows of shade-trees on each side,—the houses exhaling freshness and cleanliness, the impure and miasmatic gases and vapors being carried away and disinfected by the currents of fresh air continually rising as it becomes rarefied,—and then look at our present cities, with their utter want of arboreal beauty or cleanliness, their narrow streets, their blind-alleys, their smoking furnace-stacks, and their ill-constructed houses, emitting the most deadly poison every morning, when the surcharge accumulated during the night seeks egress! Life can be made very beautiful, but it is the law that must furnish the first condition, by compelling the selfishness of man to yield up ample spaces on the surface of the earth for arboreal ventilation and aerial purification, so necessary to preserve the health, happiness, and strength of the people.

One would suppose, from the way our cities and villages are laid out and our houses are built, that there is not a sufficient supply of land in the republic to furnish the inhabitants room to draw one breath of pure air. When thieving despots had full sway, when tribes, races, and nations were continually at war with each other, the cities were diminished in extent as much as possible, and surrounded by fortified walls; but now the improvements in the implements of war render such obstructions of no avail against well-appointed armies, and the fate of nations is determined by conflicts in the open field. It will, I hope, no longer be necessary to crowd the inhabitants of cities and villages within narrow limits and massive fortifications to protect them and their property from marauding and plundering emperors, despots, kings, dukes, or other military robbers. I believe that a new era is dawning upon the enlightened nations of the world, an era of liberty and law united in their synthesis of political justice, wherein states may be founded and cities built upon rational principles of sanitary science, and the inherent right of each citizen to pure air, pure food, pure drinks, and healthy recreation, will be protected and enforced by the laws of each State in all federative republics.

It has been objected that these necessary sanitary improvements will be very expensive. Can we not afford to be healthy, pure, and happy when all the means to become so are, as it were, in our own hands? Such parsimony that would rob the people of all that is valuable in life on the score of economy should be coupled with that prodigality which lately led Congress to give away to railroad monopolies over one hundred million acres of land belonging to the people of the United States.

II. PUBLIC EDUCATION.

CHAPTER I.

RELATION OF MORALITY AND LAW.

THE conception of law has a twofold peculiarity. It is that of a power and knowledge that lies wholly beyond nature, for nature has made no provision against the interference of one man's freedom and activity with the freedom and activity of the other, but leaves to man every possibility of killing, injuring, and checking the freedom of his fellow-man.

Nor is the conception of law that of a moral force, for the moral law, manifesting itself as a command to realize the highest good and happiness, addresses itself to each member of the moral world with categorical necessity and in perfect harmony. All men have the same common moral as they have the same common physical world, so that the moral acts of all necessarily and of themselves harmonize into one. The moral law, therefore, does not need the conception of right or wrong to enforce itself, and were its rule established the power of law would be no longer necessary.

But the moral law cannot manifest and enforce itself except in beings that have already developed themselves into freedom and morality; and it is this that gives rise to the conception of right and law as the intermediate force whereby men are to be enabled to develop their freedom, under the law, to a degree that shall make possible the supreme rules of morality.

It is this moral law, this world of an absolute and universal good, that each individual should aspire to realize in his own person, and in the subduing of all evil, with its consequent physical ailments; and it is only in thus subjecting himself to the greatest good that the individual first becomes truly free, giving highest form of expression through his works to the inspirations drawn from it and the intuitions of its grandeur, truth, and beauty. It is thus through a system of individual moral beings that the highest good is reflected in an infinite manner of different stand-points of beauty, and that within his one world of unlimited glory God has created infinite universes through the different mirrorings, translations, and intuitions of each individual: every monad reflecting in a new beautiful way the glory of the highest. It is thus that from the divine fountain of love and goodness endless inspirations of beauty and truth ripple forth with circles of wondrous perspectives, evermore extending the power of the human mind for the attainment of its highest destination and its greatest good and happiness.

CHAPTER II.

THE RIGHT TO REST.

It is through law that man is to rise to this state; the law is to be the intermediate agency between man's primitive natural condition and his ideal as a fitly- and harmoniously-developed exponent of the highest good, or as a completely free being; for in complete freedom this highest good finds its expression. This freedom he aspires to attain; to secure it, and for no other purpose, does man establish law and a state organization, and no state organization has any claim to be tolerated which does not provide for securing this freedom. No man to whom the means of realizing this, his destination, are denied by a state, is bound to obey it; the state not having respected his rights, he cannot respect it.

In wisest forethought the great legislator of antiquity, Moses, set apart one out of every seven days for the purpose of securing time to worship God and to attain moral culture to even the meanest of slave-laborers; and it is a disgrace to our age that we are not yet further advanced, and that countless men and women are still forced to work all days, so that night brings no leisure for the development of their higher natures, and Sunday scarcely a few hours of time necessary for physical recreation. Nay, in how many manufacturing districts are not even young children thus locked out by slavish labor from development and education!

The state should, by law, establish a minimum quantity of time, to be secured to children and adults respectively, for the development of their higher natures and the exercise of their real freedom. It is the time thus secured which really establishes the true wealth of a man. Not in proportion as he has gold and silver coins, or paper tokens of wealth, but in proportion as he has time for the culture and exercise of his true freedom, should a man be classed wealthy. His deeds of freedom are his riches; every additional hour of leisure from mere toil, every hour of spare time wherein to work out his individual share in the attainment of the highest good and happiness which a state can make accessible to its citizens, increases in that proportion the wealth of the state. It is, therefore, a contradiction of the end and aim of a state organization when a state accounts itself rich because its citizens by slavish toil produce or manufacture to exorbitant degrees. It is the relief from such inordinate toil that constitutes wealth.

In an unconscious sort of way this truth has manifested itself in various labor-movements, both here and in Europe; but it is a truth which should not be rendered abortive by crude advocacy and the one-sidedness of a class, but which the state itself should announce as the fundamental principle of its laws governing labor, money, and property.

Since Sunday is by the great majority of the people of the United States recognized as the fit and appropriate day for such rest, the law should make that day sacred to rest, instruction, and moral contemplation by forbidding absolutely all kinds of labor, so that not a single one of the citizens may have reason to complain that he has not time for the cultivation of his higher faculties and nature, of his social qualities, and for the recreation of his mind and body.

CHAPTER III.

THE RIGHT TO SCHOOLS.

It is not sufficient, however, that the state should provide the requisite time for the attainment of culture; it must also provide the means necessary to realize this: whereby the state will attach all its citizens to a pure obedience to the laws and prove that the government established to secure the greatest good, happiness, morality, intelligence, wisdom, and perfection of its citizens, is the best and surest friend of each person in the state. In this way will each one learn to love the law which affords him such absolute protection, and secures him in the enjoyment of all his rights and the development of all his faculties.

These means are schools, institutions for the harmonious development of all our faculties to the utmost possible perfection, and of clear insight into all the problems of life, so that the darkness and superstition accompanying ignorance, which are the main obstacles to the development of man's freedom, may be forever swept away from the face of the world.

CHAPTER IV.

THE NATURE OF EDUCATION.

Everything moves by law, as in the physical so in the intellectual and moral world: both worlds in perfect harmony and accord. It is the chief task of education to awaken and cultivate an insight into this lawfulness of all phenomena, so that the world of mind and inner soul may no longer seem to clash with and oppose the world of nature, but be found to move to the same measures and tunes, and that the smallest event in the physical world be seen to fall into perfect harmony with the plan and events of the moral world. Thus the world of nature will no longer appear man's antagonist, but his friend and home, as it has not yet been in any age, and develop supernal radiance as expressing, under man's constantly extending control and dominion, the wonders of the intellectual and moral universe, which the people of former ages believed were hidden by nature; while, on the other hand, the creative power of the intellectual and moral universe will illumine all with new and ever-growing and varying beauties; even as the body of man is beautified by his moral and intellectual nature in the progress of civilization, making the body and mind of the civilized man of culture reflect the glory of the divinity with infinitely greater splendor than it is ever seen in the body and mind of the uncultured savage.

Thus in the studies of mathematics, physics, natural history, and medicine, the teacher will develop a knowledge of the manifold phenomena of nature, point out their separate laws and the harmony and correlation of these laws, and show how all laws have been provided for by the phenomena in an absolute intelligence, and continue so to be provided as new orders of phenomena are made known and present themselves for classification.

In the studies of history, geography, politics, law, social science, and philology, the teacher will, on the other hand, point out in the course of human civilization, with all its attainments in art and culture, the proportionate growth of the highest good and happiness, and how it moves in rhythmic movements and symmetrical proportions towards the establishment of its ideal.

Finally, in the study of philosophy, the science of all sciences, the teacher will teach the source of all knowledge in an examination of even that knowledge itself, its nature and condition, thus making known the source of all truth, since all truth is a knowledge and the fountain of the fundamental principles of each special science and branch of knowledge. In this highest of all sciences the last veil shall fall from the mind of the scholar, and the whole universe appear to him in full clearness.

But the teacher is not only to unfold to the intellect the wonders of the universe and exhibit their harmonious relation, he is also to teach the pupil the course of action he is to perform in this world, his practical duty,—firstly, in regard to himself: the vocation he may choose in active life, and to purify and cleanse his own mind and body, so that he will be fit to attain the greatest good and happiness in the pursuit of that vocation of which his faculties are susceptible; and secondly, in regard to others, that the ultimate as well as the present greatest good and happiness of all men must of necessity be always the aim and object of each man, and that men must love the law, by means of which alone this is made possible.

This opens up the studies of ethics, morals, and æsthetics, or of intuition and inspiration, studies now altogether neglected in public education, and yet so essential to the development of man's higher nature, which requires such development with paramount necessity in our age of materialistic tendencies and mammon-worship.

With this high view of the faculties of man, the resurrected notion of man's descent from the ape and the survival of the fittest can, of course, have little in common. Based upon the altogether unsupported national economical theory of Malthus that population increases in a geometrical proportion, while the means of life increase only in arithmetical proportion, and that thus only a few have the means to survive, this notion would make us believe what no history of facts ever has demonstrated or can demonstrate, that in the grand war for existence only the highest developments can survive. All history shows this assertion to be a pure fiction and metaphysical coinage of the brain. The highest civilizations have perished, and the rudest of Africa and Asia have survived. All history of natural phenomena contradicts it, as Cuvier demonstrated already in 1830, when he showed that so far as historical experience extends no transition of one type of organisms into another is traceable; the ibis on the monuments of Egypt is the same as the ibis of to-day; the earliest sculptured form of man is precisely what it is now. It is not so difficult to comprehend how God made man. But it is utterly beyond the power of mind to understand how an ape produced man; and the greatest anatomist of England, Huxley, has, moreover, shown that there are differences in the structure of man and that of any known kind of ape, which make it easy to detect at a glance to which species the bones belong.

Indeed, so far as all historical knowledge extends,—and it is pure metaphysical subtlety to speculate beyond that,—man has always exhibited the same high faculties that he possesses to-day, has always been capable of the same development of those faculties, and always been subject to the same earthly end of them—death. Nowhere is there an historical instance of apes changed into men, nowhere an historical instance of men transformed into other creatures. Man may live forever and forever and he will still be man; the ape may continue for millions of years and he will still be an ape.

Permanence and development of the permanent are the two everlasting opposites of the universe, and their synthesis is reached in education. The infinity of life that we are sure to live in the everlasting life beyond the grave will still leave us men, the same men we were on this earth, with all our memories of its manifold sweetnesses and inexpressible sorrows. Far more perfect we shall be, no doubt, growing beyond our highest expectations in goodness, happiness, beauty, and wisdom, and yet will be neither transmigrated into beasts, as Pythagoras taught, nor submerged into God, as Brahma fancied, but remain forever men, to whatever grander heights of development we may be raised above our present.

CHAPTER V.

CLASSIFICATION OF SCHOOLS.

As a means to all these studies, the body of the student must be taught—first, generally in gymnasiums, for the development of its fullest health and strength, and agility of its limbs; and second, specifically for the development of the various senses and organs, according as the pupil may need for his chosen vocation in life.

Thus schools have a threefold function:

1. To develop the body so as to make it in every respect a complete, healthy, diligent, and well-trained expression and instrument of the soul and mind.

2. To develop all the faculties of the mind, and all senses and organs of the body, according as the pupil may choose his vocation in life, for the perception and realization in himself and all others of the highest good and happiness.

3. To develop the moral faculty, or knowledge of, reverence for, and implicit subjection to, the idea of the highest good.

And a complete system of schools involves the establishment of—

SCHOOLS FOR PHYSICAL EDUCATION.

GYMNASIUMS, with MILITARY SCHOOLS attached to them, for the development of the body and instruction in military practice, which are to be attached to all the following schools except the university:

SCHOOLS FOR INTELLECTUAL EDUCATION.

1. Common schools—for teaching the first elementary branches, and graded so as to prepare the pupil for either one of the following:

2. Agricultural schools—comprising botany, landscape arboriculture, pomology, gardening, vegetable chemistry, geology, zoology, and surveying.

3. Industrial schools—for teaching all kinds of industrial labors and works, and the secret arts of the trades.

4. Schools of technology or useful arts—wherein are to be taught civil and military engineering, mechanical engineering, geology, and mining engineering, building, engraving, photographing, telegraphing, navigation, and astronomy.

5. Schools of fine art—for educating artists in the various fine arts: painting, sculpture, architecture in its character as art, music, and poetry.

6. High schools—where the higher branches will be taught, preparing pupils, according as they may choose their vocation in life, for either of the following:

7. Normal schools—to be established exclusively for the education of teachers.

8. Business schools—for the education of pupils in all classes of business: manufacturing, commerce, banking, and office business.

9. Law schools—for the education of lawyers.

10. Schools of medicine—for the education of doctors and surgeons.

11. Colleges—where the highest branches of all knowledge and science are to be taught, so as to raise a corps of men devoted exclusively to culture and science for—

12. The university.

Education of the moral faculty to be a part of the duties and purposes of every school, except the gymnasium and the university.

CHAPTER VI.

SCHOOL EXHIBITIONS.

It will be well to arrange for each school a system of rewards or premiums, by means of which to incite the scholars to unremitting effort and awaken their sense of honor, which is the same as their self-respect, whereof Kant says that it is the ultimate basis of all morality.

For the common schools this can be easily arranged by the distribution of medals for morality, industry, learning, and good behavior, and by other tokens of approval and rewards, which have a far happier effect in inciting the scholar to increased effort than punishments, that only degrade him in his own eyes, and by thus lessening his self-respect undermine his whole moral nature.

The agricultural schools should have annual exhibitions in every county, in which all the farmers of the county might join in annual fairs, where scholars and practical farmers would meet together and interchange thoughts, experiences, and learning, and where the teachers of the agricultural schools might distribute medals of reward both among their own scholars according to their respective proficiency, and among the farmers according to the results of their respective labors, thus encouraging and stimulating a healthy rivalry and spirit to excel in producing the very best of that kind of vegetable and animal food with which the welfare of all citizens is so intimately connected.

The industrial and technological schools might, where it is practicable, unite with the agricultural schools in a common exhibition, making mutually known to each other what has been accomplished by either in their separate branches, and uniting in common festivities.

The same system of rewards should be applied to all other schools, and it would be well if the state should take appreciative cognizance of the moral conduct of its citizens by acknowledging rare acts of self-devotion, philanthropy, and charity.

In this way the fundamental principle of our organic code, that the true end and aim of all government is to attain the highest good, happiness, and wisdom for the individual and each of his neighbors, would be steadily deeper engrafted into the hearts of the citizens, and men would cease to regard the attainment of a position of power, position, place, or of superfluous wealth as their proper aim in life. The curse of American civilization, love of such power, place, and wealth, and sacrifice of all noble ends in life to their attainment, would be eradicated, or at least greatly diminished.

CHAPTER VII.

THE EDUCATION OF EVERY SCHOLAR FOR A VOCATION.

To perceive and realize for himself and others the greatest good and happiness in a state, each pupil in early life must choose a vocation, and in the above system of schools each pupil will be enabled to prepare himself for the vocation he chooses, and thus to enter life fully equipped with means to earn his livelihood immediately after his education is completed. Nor need he spend any time in studies that are not necessary for his vocation and general culture, and will thus be enabled all the better to learn the particular vocation of his choice. The pupil, for instance, who aspires to become a lawyer, can, immediately after passing through the common school and high school,—in which latter he can select only such studies as will be beneficial to him for his profession and general culture,—go to the law school; while the one who wishes to become a farmer can, immediately after having passed the common school, advance to the agricultural school.

In order to make this education accessible to every member of the state, and to furnish each person with the necessary knowledge and dexterity demanded by his vocation, thereby making pauperism impossible, the state must furnish to each pupil lodging, food, and clothing during the term of his scholarship.

This will, of course, be done only when it is necessary and required; but by doing it such institutions as work-houses will be rendered altogether useless, and an effectual stop put to the spread of crime. The expense will be comparatively slight, and saved thousands of times in doing away with the institutions now found necessary to erect and support for paupers and criminals, and which, by the peculiar degradatory character attached to them, keep permanent a peculiar and constantly increasing class of indigents, the dangerous element of every society.

In all agricultural districts and smaller villages and cities, for instance, there will be only few children and young persons who will require the support of the state during the time of their education; and it is only in the larger cities that expensive measures will have to be adopted. The immense majority of parents will always prefer to provide their children themselves with raiment and food. But by providing those who are unable to do this with the means of education, and furnishing the poorest child with an education, profession, or trade, the state will for the first time in history have realized the doctrine of human equality in its full and true sense, by placing into the hands of every citizen a livelihood. For the other distinction of life, which results from money, is but accidental, and of no value to him who has the means of earning enough for his living, with the capacity of self-development placed equally in his hands.

It is, of course, understood that all classes of education are open equally to both sexes. In the lowest class of schools, as well as in the highest, the university, both sexes may use, moreover, the same schools; in all intermediate schools different ones will have to be arranged for either sex. In women's working schools, of course, women only are to be admitted.

CHAPTER VIII.

ANALYSIS OF THIS SYSTEM OF SCHOOLS.

I WILL now enter upon a more detailed account of the several classes of schools, and their peculiar character.

GYMNASIUMS.

In gymnasiums the body in general is to be educated into flexible obedience to the will of its possessor. As everything in the double world of nature and spirit moves in obedience to harmonious laws, so the culture of the body, as an instrument of the mind, infuses health into the physical and mental organization; and the gymnasium is, therefore, both a sanitary and an educational institution, and its teacher or teachers must be competent in both respects.

By nature the human body is a mere mass of organs, clumsy, shapeless, and disobedient; not a fixed, determined organization like the body of an animal, but the indefinite, undetermined organization of a rational being, who is to work it out himself, a body with no other character than that of determinability. Physical education is to take hold of this clumsy body and make of it the most artistic object in the universe, irradiating beauty by its glow and proportions, as well as by the grace of its movements, and revealing the most developed strength and agility in each of its limbs. Wonderful quickness and power are to be developed in every part of the body, a strength and security of movement which seem almost supernatural, and the obedience of every limb is to be no longer sullen and slow, but quick and dexterous.

To attain this development of the body, teachers must be selected that are well instructed in all the appliances of the science of gymnastics, and with competent knowledge of the sanitary effects of the various kinds of gymnastical evolutions upon the body. One of the most beautiful exercises, imparting grace of movement, and, at the same time, enjoyable in a high degree, is dancing, which should, therefore, be taught in every gymnasium. Nor should this exercise be confined to the common dances, but reach to the highest branches of the art of dancing, wherein the movements of the body become the visible interpreters of the movements of the music.

To every gymnasium there should also be attached a swimming school, so that this healthy and refreshing exercise, a knowledge of which may so often preserve life, should be acquired by as many scholars as possible.

With bodies thus developed into health, strength, and grace, and wherein the mind would exercise that instantaneous and perfect control and force which is the result of such development, the men and women of the country would rise to a condition of self-reliance, strength, pride, and glory such as speaks to us through the finest statues of ancient Greece. Health and litheness would make every moment of life a delight and joy.

MILITARY SCHOOLS.

If history emphasizes any fact it is this, that nothing is more fatal to the political liberties of the people of a state than the organization of an exclusive, distinct military body; and the more numerous such a body is the greater will be the oppression. Even where such a military body is organized among the people themselves, and for only temporary service and drill, as is the case in Germany under the landwehr system, the evil effects are directly apparent. Horrible as the object itself is for which military drill is needed, the spirit inculcated by the drill bears even worse results; for while war only destroys life, the spirit of submission and dependence which is infused by the drill, and which gradually prepares men for a condition of slavery in general, destroys all that gives value to life. Hence all countries have drifted more and more into political slavery as their standing armies were increased; and in Germany especially such abandonment of formerly free and republican principles and feelings among the people for slavish subjection to imperial rule has patently been the result of its system of a military force which enlists every citizen, and thereby infects the whole population of the state with that military slavish spirit.

Nevertheless, the time has not yet come when, under such an international code as I shall propose, the military body of a state can be entirely dispensed with. We, meanwhile, need a small professionally military force for naval and garrison duty, and at the same time we need another larger force that shall make us at all times prepared to levy against any foreign power all the strength, art, and science of our government. For it is the most perfect state, the state of fullest individual freedom and least despotic power, which is in greatest danger of attack from the despotism of other countries, as most likely by its example to arouse their people to a struggle for a similar condition of liberty under the law.

The problem is, therefore, so to arrange matters that our government shall have at all times ready all the resources of the art of war, and all the forces of the republic, without having a specially organized military body, except the small one heretofore mentioned.

So far as the instruments of war are concerned there need be no difficulty. Fortifications can be built, and kept in condition of defense, according to the most advanced principles of military science, without endangering the liberties of the people. Ships of war also can be constructed in sufficient number, and the necessary material of war for all branches of the service can always be kept on hand.

So far as the men, the soldiers, are concerned, it seems to me that if the gymnasium were to add to its course of instruction a course of military drill, the main body of an army, the infantry, would at all times be on hand. Such a government as I propose, with a body of men physically developed in every respect by the gymnasium, and, moreover, practiced in the drill of military service, needs no further special organization of that body to render it effective at any time. The men of the state would all be as conversant with the drill of the service as with their A, B, C's, ready at any moment to apply their knowledge; and yet they would be without any organization until the moment of peril.

The cavalry branch of the army, which is comparatively of small importance, could be formed in cities. Requiring, as it does, the drilling of horses besides the drilling of men, and the exercise of large numbers at one time, it would be, perhaps, inconvenient to collect in the country a sufficient force at one time for the purpose of military training. But among the young men of the cities attending the gymnasium a sufficient number could doubtless be collected to organize for instruction in cavalry practice, more especially as the exercises would necessarily take them out in the open country, and thus combine recreation and enjoyment with military instruction.

Artillery practice might also be taught in large cities, but particularly in the districts adjoining fortifications and navy-yards. This branch of the service is of the least importance in actual battle, for its main effect is to produce fear by noise, and a proper degree of individual courage on the part of the infantry is always able to overcome it. Machiavelli pointed this out long ago, and wherever a fearless and educated infantry has been opposed to artillery the result has corroborated his judgment.

In this manner the state would have ready at all times an effective service, without the dangerous element of a specially organized military body. Against such an army of active, healthy, well-drilled, and intelligent freemen no other army of equal numbers could long hold out. And it is to be hoped that the international judiciary proposed in my system for the final settlement of all questions at issue between kingdoms, empires, and republics belonging to the international federative association of civilized, enlightened nations, will enable them to settle all disputes without resorting to war.

COMMON PUBLIC SCHOOLS.

In the common public schools the child gets its first control over the instruments of all learning: reading, writing, and ciphering. Having acquired this control, the child is, by a judicious system of gradation, taught to apply those instruments in the acquirement of a knowledge of fundamental history, geography, natural history, and, finally, perhaps the first principles of natural philosophy and chemistry.

In order to accomplish the most in the least time, the hours of school-attendance should be as few as possible; but the corps of teachers should be as large as practicable, so that each teacher may have but a small number of children under his direct supervision. It is surely not necessary to keep children at exercises that tire their eyes and weary their young bodies merely to while time away; nor is it policy to intrust to one teacher more children than he can pay attention to. In Prussia, for instance, there is only one school-teacher for every forty scholars; and yet that same state thinks it necessary to employ one teacher, called corporal, for every *six* military scholars or soldiers.

Needing only a few hours' attendance per day at the common school, the child will have ample time for the art school and the gymnasium, and yet have abundant leisure for play, recreation, training, and self-culture at home.

From the common public school the child can enter the agricultural school, or the industrial school, or the school of technology, or, if it decides to pursue a higher education, it may enter the high school.

AGRICULTURAL SCHOOLS.

Agriculture, being the most independent profession, in that it furnishes man directly his food and the materials for clothing, will probably be at all times the chosen vocation of the proportionately larger number of scholars, and should, indeed, be encouraged, rewarded, and made profitable in every way. The main problem of agriculture is to gain the greatest amount of the various products from the least amount of land without deteriorating the soil;

and in proportion as the state increases in population the importance of this problem becomes greater, as will be shown more particularly hereafter when speaking of the vast amounts of lands squandered upon the railroads through the recklessness of Congress.

The scholar who chooses agriculture for his vocation must be instructed in all the means science has discovered to solve that problem, and at the same time be made partially conversant with the appliances of labor whereby to carry them out.

For the latter purpose it is absolutely necessary that every agricultural school should be situated upon an extensive tract of land, whereon the various forms of agriculture can be carried out. Part of the land will therefore have to be laid out in a farm; part in forests, orchards, and vineyards; part in pasturage; part in useful vegetable gardens, and part in artistic landscape and gardens.

The scholars may be assigned to either branch of the work, or, if their stay at school is long enough, to more or all of them.

For the former purpose it is necessary to set apart certain hours of the day for instruction in the various sciences relating to agriculture, as, for instance, chemistry of the soil, vegetable chemistry, manuring, stock-raising, pomology, botany, landscape gardening, grafting, geology, and zoology.

To these studies should be added lectures for the development of moral culture and culture in general, —the secluded life of the farmer making it essential to his happiness that he should acquire a taste for the fine arts in their various forms,—and also a series of lectures on the constitution and laws of the state and of the federative system.

INDUSTRIAL SCHOOLS.

Of the pupils of those schools who do not choose agriculture for their vocation, a number will doubtless engage in industrial pursuits, and should therefore be fitted out by the state with all the knowledge necessary for that purpose in special industrial schools, with separate schools for the instruction of women in labors and acquirements that are purely womanly.

The industrial schools for boys should provide and teach all kinds of work and manufacture practiced in the state, as the taste of the scholar may single out for his vocation. These schools, as well as the agricultural schools, can be made productive, and the profits divided among the pupils and used for premiums. Still, it should on no account be the object of the schools to be made productive for the state, since such a system would surely lead to oppression and corruption, and excite dissatisfaction among the scholars.

The industrial schools for women should educate girls in all the work peculiar to housekeeping, and all other kinds of work that may belong peculiarly to women, as sewing, embroidery, knitting, etc. At the same time they should be allowed and encouraged to learn any of the other kinds of industrial work that any one might desire to choose for her livelihood, as telegraphing, printing, etc. But, as the art of housekeeping, with its various elements, will in some way or another need to be known by every woman, special attention should be devoted to this branch of the school. All matters relating to the kitchen, the chemistry of cooking, the sanitary and gastronomical elements of diet, and its rotation during the week and the seasons of the year, should be thoroughly taught; as also the mode of keeping accounts for the household, etc.

In both classes of industrial schools a course of general culture and literature should accompany the specific instruction, and also, as indeed in every school, a course of lectures on the constitution and laws of the state and of the federation.

SCHOOLS OF TECHNOLOGY.

Schools of technology have already been established in one or two of our States, but every State should have at least one. In these schools all the mechanical professions and the studies connected with them: physics, chemistry, thermo-dynamics, machinery, metallurgy, mineralogy, engineering, surveying, mining, engraving, photographing, telegraphing, and navigation.

As all these sciences are based upon mathematics, their study will have to be made a specialty in the schools of technology, as also the study of astronomy, which is indispensable for several of the branches taught.

Architecture, being not only an art, but also an

engineering profession, should also be taught in this its character, as building, in the technological institutes. This includes the teaching of architectural design and drawing, construction and applied mechanics, the chemistry of building materials, etc.

As the government will have to rely upon the graduates of the schools of technology to supply its military officers in times of war, the study of military engineering, surveying, and of all matters appertaining to military science, should be made a special department.

A course of instruction in general culture should also in these schools accompany the technical course of study, and should embrace the studies of modern languages, history, botany, and composition.

SCHOOLS OF FINE ARTS.

In the widest sense of the word, every work of the human intelligence, as a manifestation of its creative power in contradistinction from the works of nature, might properly be termed a work of art; but usage has limited the use of that phrase to those works that have no other design than to exhibit man's creative power, and has signified the limitation by speaking of the arts generally as fine arts, although one of them, architecture, branches over into the useful.

But all other fine arts have only the beautiful for their object: the beautiful, which is love; the love, which is creativeness. Every rational being loves by its very nature to create, and the love of art is therefore universal. It is to be expected that every pupil of all the other schools will apply for admission to the school of arts for the purpose of learning some one favorite art, which he can practice in the leisure hours of his future life, so that he may be able to fill up spare moments for himself and those around him with the enjoyment of pure beauty.

But quite a number of scholars, to whom nature has kindly given a peculiar talent for some one of the arts, will wish to obtain a perfect education in the art chosen, with a view of making it their future vocation. These latter constitute a class of artists proper, while the former are only amateurs.

For the artistic education of amateurs it will suffice to set apart one or two hours of study in the school of arts, while they are pursuing their regular studies in the other schools to which they may belong. These hours might be arranged for the evenings.

The pursuit of art being itself an enjoyment and pleasure, its study will not overtax the physical strength of any scholar, but rather recuperate it. Each amateur scholar must, of course, be at liberty to choose the art he desires to practice, or to choose two, if he has the necessary time and energy. It is of the greatest practical value for the future enjoyment of life that every pupil of any school should acquire at least one art thoroughly, so that his taste for beauty may be sufficiently developed to appreciate it in every form.

Those who desire to make a special vocation of some one particular art will, of course, make the school of arts their permanent home during their term of instruction. All the materials necessary for their studies should be furnished by the state. The art productions that are sold would amply reimburse the outlay. The remaining profit should, of course, go to the respective artists.

Music being of all arts the one most easily practiced under all circumstances of life, and the one most effective in amusing and in developing man's moral nature, because it appeals most intensely to his internality, should be taught in some one of its forms, and as much as practicable, to every child. It was surely not without having observed this its effect that the Greeks laid such stress upon it as an educational agent.

HIGH SCHOOLS.

The high schools take up education at the point where the common schools leave off, and pursue it in all its branches; each pupil, however, receiving only such education as his future vocation in life may demand. Those who wish to become business men, for instance, receive another course of instruction than those who desire to devote their lives to pure science, or to any one of the sciences, as philology, mathematics, etc. For it is not only useless but positively injurious to teach scholars matters that they cannot pursue in their future career in life. A smattering of Latin and Greek taught to a boy who intends to enter business life both takes his time and mind away from the studies he should pursue, and fills him with false conceit. Every citizen of the state should have his special function, and learn to be completely master of that, and not attempt to fill his mind with a little undigested knowledge of things that lie beyond his sphere.

The pupils who have passed through their course of study at the high schools should then be allowed to choose either of the following for the completion of their education:

NORMAL SCHOOLS.

The normal schools should be exclusively adapted and established for the education of teachers; and it is absolutely necessary that there should be such schools to train teachers for their special profession. The science of pedagogics or teaching has to be studied just as well as any other science, or we shall never get a body of teachers fit to take charge of the various schools of the state, and conversant with their art in all its branches and details. The normal schools are intended to educate a corps of teachers whose sole aim in life it shall be to teach, who shall consider this their permanent vocation, and devote all their skill and energy to carry on teaching successfully. The shifting body of teachers to whom we commonly intrust our schools, who take up the profession of teaching simply from temporary necessity, and who have to learn their science in the schools themselves, must be altogether dispensed with. Only when this is accomplished can we rid ourselves of the text-book system, with the mechanical drill it inculcates, and which deadens the minds of the pupils, checking every development of freedom and individuality.

Every teacher should be competent to teach without a text-book, whether it be history, geography, natural history, or any of the sciences, and should have learned the art of teaching so impressively that in conversation with his pupils, drawing them out and causing them to originate their own answers, instead of memorizing from the text-book the answer that is expected, he will illustrate all principles taught.

It is only by such a mode of teaching that a teacher will ever succeed in making his pupil think for himself, and comprehend thoroughly the reason of the matter taught, so that he shall be able in all his future life to remember it and apply it practically to any problem that may be sprung upon him.

BUSINESS SCHOOLS.

As things are at present, those children who desire to enter commercial, banking, manufacturing, or office life, do so unprepared by any especial instruction furnished them in our public schools. They thus have to learn whatever business they choose altogether by experience,—a very slow and uncertain school with indifferent teachers, not very remunerative either, since the salary of the inexperienced is necessarily small; a circumstance that is a fruitful source of crime.

Under the system of schools herein proposed, the pupil who aspires to a life of business will not be required to study a number of matters that are utterly useless for him in his future vocation, but enter from the high school directly into the business school, and there be taught—

1. Whatever pertains to manufacturing or commercial life; the nature and native places of the various articles of commerce, their mode of transportation, cost, insurance, etc.; and all these matters should be taught as they are at the time, so that the scholar may enter the world of commerce with a knowledge of the present and not of a practically useless past. The art of book-keeping must, of course, be taught, so also correspondence, and when, required, modern languages.

2. Banking in all its branches, its history and growth, and the science of money and finances.

3. All kinds of office business, such as insurance, real estate, notarial duties, and such other office business as may be carried on in the state.

LAW SCHOOLS.

In every school a course of general instruction concerning the laws and constitution of the state and federation should be given; but in the law schools this instruction is to be special and for the purpose of training a corps of lawyers, judges, and statesmen that shall be reliable and efficient.

Only such persons as have finished the course of study at these schools and received a diploma should be allowed to practice law and be elective for the judiciary department of the state and federation, so that no citizen may receive injury from incompetent judges or by employing incompetent counsel.

The study of pure law should be accompanied by a course of the history of law and government in the various forms they have assumed in the development of the human race. Thus besides the study of the organic law of the state and of the federal government, of the state and federal codes, civil and criminal, there should be a course on the codes of foreign countries, on the principles of common law and equity, on ancient, feudal, and civil law, and finally, on international law and international jurisprudence.

It must be borne in mind that the law schools are to educate not only judges and lawyers,—that is to say servants and interpreters of existing law,—but also legislators,—the makers of law,—and that hence there should be taught not only the existing and historical statutes and forms of law, but also the fundamental principles of law and government. These fundamental principles of the science of law and their deduction from the fundamental principles of knowledge in general will be furnished by the university, through its professors of philosophy.

SCHOOLS OF MEDICINE AND SURGERY.

No one should be allowed to practice medicine in a state who has not passed the medical school and received a diploma; and no person should be allowed to sell drugs or medicines unless he has passed through the pharmacy department of these schools and received a proper certificate.

As the whole science of medicine, so far as it depends upon the effects of drugs, is purely experimental, all systems of practice should be equally taught; and for the same reason a record should be kept and arranged under a proper system to show the direct results that have followed the administration of any medicine. No science being so purely negative and dependent upon experiment as the science of medicine, it is of the utmost importance to have a continuous record of all experiments made with any kind of drug,—allopathic or homœopathic,—or with any kind of mixture and the compounds of that mixture; and such record, together with all other facts regarding diseases, the spread of epidemics, etc., should periodically be made public.

Surgery, dentistry, diseases of the eyes and ears, and indeed all diseases which require mechanical treatment, should constitute special departments of the science of medicine, since these diseases certainly admit a purely scientific treatment.

COLLEGES.

Under the above-sketched system of schools, there will be left for entrance into college life only those young men or women who desire to devote themselves altogether to science.

The high school does not propose to educate its pupils any further than to fit them for entrance into the schools just named; and hence, to raise them to a standard of education which alone will make them valuable members of the university, the college must step in as the mediating factor. The college is to furnish to such persons the highest culture attainable to each one in the special department of science he may choose: mathematics, physics, natural history, geography, astronomy, philology, history, æsthetics, etc.

Having passed through the college, the student has served his apprenticeship of learning, and, becoming a master, enters into full and equal intercourse with all other men of science by means of the university.

UNIVERSITIES.

The university is to be, not so much a school,—that is, a place for teaching,—as rather a place for the appliance and further new development of the highest grade of learning, the gathering-place of the chief men of the various sciences, and of all who desire to devote their life exclusively to science, for common intercourse and improvement, the central point from which each state, in conjunction with the universities of all other states, is to carry on the ultimate aim of all states: to subjugate nature to the highest attainable extent unto the control and directive power of men, and to develop the highest culture and clearness in men, thereby realizing their greatest good and happiness.

Here the most perfect instruments in this war of subjugation should be collected and arranged; here constant experiments and observations be conducted, and the result of all other private and public experiments and observations be gathered and reported again to all other universities and institutions, as may be requisite; here the most complete libraries, art-galleries, museums, etc., should be established, and here finally the teachers of the highest science, of philosophy, should find their sphere of action opening up its treasures to the highest-developed minds, and giving, from its universal form and substance, to every other science its fundamental principles and the form of its procedure.

In this way all universities of the world may gradually form an organized body of all the world's learning and knowledge, each separate one a nucleus and representation of all, and reflecting back upon all its own additional light and acquirement, realizing Leibnitz's great conception of an organized body of scientific men over the whole earth, working together disinterestedly for one common object, and each one doing the peculiar work assigned to him, so that no valuable time and labor may be lost in having the same thing done by many, as occurs constantly under the present unorganized system of things.

A state having such a university, and giving the best scholars of the country there assembled proper communication and influence with that part of the state organization for which they may be respectively specially qualified, would soon achieve results to excite the admiration and emulation of all its neighbors. With such a trained corps of scientific men, physical disease and hereditary maladies could doubtless be almost annihilated, the forces of nature tamed and regulated beyond the most sanguine dreams of this day, and the finances and property laws of the state so codified as to secure law, order, justice, happiness, and prosperity.

For the power of man is infinite, and when he once opens his eyes to see clearly, he will discover means and remedies for every evil that afflicts the race. The superstitious notions of the past on all matters of religion, or law, or medicine, or social and political organization, being once removed, it will become apparent that the distrust in his own perfectibility on the part of man was unfounded, and that every problem of the race is capable of solution and must be solved, and that it could not be a problem given to the race by the Divinity had not the race the power to solve it.

There is no necessity for misery, crime, and disease, and a social and political organization can and must be invented that will prevent them; there is no necessity for living in dread of the forces of nature, and measures must be discovered by which to overcome them; there is no necessity for the spiritual gloom and fears that send so many to insane asylums and premature graves, and a science of all knowledge must remove the last remnant of darkness from men's minds and spread everywhere and over all time spiritual and intellectual light and clearness, developing the true inspirations.

To make these discoveries, organize these measures, and spread this light, and thus to realize the highest good, wisdom, happiness, and perfection for all inhabitants of the state, should be the task of the universities; and as they will be established by the state organizations herein proposed, one of the main objects of its teachers will necessarily be to perfect the organic laws of this system, and recommend an extension of its harmonious working as experience may determine, for the preservation of the rights and liberties of men for all time to come.

III. PUBLIC INTERCOMMUNICATION.

GENERAL PRINCIPLES.

I.

HAVING shown the duties of the government in regard to the preservation of the physical health, and the development of the intellectual powers of its citizens, in order to prepare them for the fit and harmonious use of all their faculties of mind and body, I shall now specify the duties of the government in regard to the intercommunication of those citizens, whereby the exercise of their social and political functions is to be protected.

That there are such duties should admit of no question. Under our own Declaration of Independence it is the purpose of government to guarantee to every citizen life, liberty, and the pursuit of happiness. But no government can make this guarantee unless it has supreme control over all the means whereby to make it valid.

These means are manifold, and, in order to make each separate one effective, should be organized into a complete and harmonious system of intercommunication. It is to be accounted one of the great deficiencies in the structure of our federative government, that this organization of the various means of intercommunication was lost sight of, or held to be beyond the proper scope of government. Hence these means drifted into separate and unconnected channels.

It is very instructive to observe the admirable systems organized by men for the management of their private business; and then notice the reckless, negligent manner in which our public affairs are administered: the former manifesting economy, industry, prudence, and activity; the latter, extravagance, idleness, and inattention. It is evident even to a casual observer that the conduct of our public administration in all matters of public intercommunication between men in our republic has allowed them to pass under the control of selfish political schemers.

When a private citizen establishes a business of any kind, he is very careful to see that each part of the work is organized so as to fit closely into all other parts; that each person employed shall have a specific portion of duties assigned him, and that the rules for the government of all these persons shall be fair and uniform in their application, clearly made known to each one and strictly enforced. But in the administration of our governmental affairs all these fundamental rules for the successful management of private business are ignored; and even this great function of government itself—to secure and promote the most reliable and economical means for universal public intercommunication between all citizens—has been surrendered and turned over to federal and State corporations, at once oppressing the people and embarrassing the government.

The federal government has divided its sovereignty over the currency of the country with national banks, in violation of the Constitution; it has invited competition with the old coin monopoly of foreign nations by impolitic discrimination in favor of gold for the payment of United States duties, compelling legal-tender notes to suffer a discount at the very time when Treasury demand notes receivable for duties were at par with coin; it has granted away its supreme control over territorial highways to federal railroad corporations created by Congress, and permits them to tax the travel and commerce on these inter-State highways without any just limitations; it has granted to telegraphic monopolies the right to control on their lines the public and private communications all over the country and across the continent, and to levy such rates of tax therefor as the corporators choose, to the great injury of the citizens and the government; and finally Congress, emboldened by the demoralizing exercise of war-powers, has boldly assumed the authority, as the law-making department, to give away the public lands to railway corporations, and the public moneys to national banking monopolies, as if its members had owned in their own right the lands and moneys belonging to the people.

Many of the State governments have also granted away portions of their sovereign powers and vast amounts of State bonds and moneys belonging to their citizens to like corporate railway monopolies, which now arrogantly seek to control those State legislatures and judiciaries as they do the federal Congress, by the corrupt use of their great money-power and influence.

All these charters and gifts, fraudulently and corruptly procured from the State and federal legislatures, should be resumed as soon as practicable by our governments; and if such corporations have acquired vested rights that cannot be divested otherwise, then the State and federal legislatures should establish regulations and rates of charges for them, to prevent their gross extortions and outrageous mismanagement, and the daily reckless destruction of human life.

It is a fundamental maxim, in the administration of a federative system of government like ours, that all the means whereby public intercommunication between the citizens of the several States and Territories is carried on, whether through a money medium, railways, telegraphs, police, or official newspapers, etc., should be subject to the exclusive control and direction of the federal and State governments, according to their respective constitutional powers and jurisdictions, so as to secure to the citizens of each State and of the United States a perfect legal equality of rights, and prevent usury and extortion.

All existing corporations in the country that interfere with or obstruct the harmonious, full, and just administration of the respective State and federal governments, established by their founders for the security and promotion of the common good and happiness of the people, should be abolished.

All existing laws tending to exempt any particular person, or combination of persons, from taxes or duties, or to create any privileged classes, corporations, or associations in any State, should be repealed.

The federal and State constitutions should be so amended that the respective legislatures should be prohibited from granting, leasing, or disposing of the whole or any portion of the sovereignty or franchises of any State; and from granting, selling, leasing, or disposing of any goods, rights, liens, lands, or things whatsoever, except upon public notice under general laws.

No village, city, township, county, or State in the republic should have any power to issue, sell, or negotiate any interest-bearing bonds, bills, or currency.

In the management of our national finances, the supreme control having been vested by the Constitution in the federal government, it is necessary for it to assume and exercise this control by enacting laws declaring what shall be the national money to the exclusion of all other money, and make a sufficient quantity to redeem all bonds and pay all debts of the republic, so as to create a circulation that will be ample for the development of industries and the requirements of trade, and at the same time free the nation from the oppressive burden of interest.

By the adoption of this policy there will be but one kind of money in the country, secured for its conversion or redemption in every article offered for sale or export, in all lands, natural wealth, products, taxes, and duties of the entire nation, now possessing larger, more available, and more valuable resources than any other in the world.

The administration of our governments, State and federal, has to a great extent ignored these general principles for the preservation of republican liberty and political equality, by permitting the growth of class legislation that is slowly but surely absorbing our common franchises and liberties, in the creation of privileged classes,—gigantic railway, banking, and telegraphic corporations,—who will at length possess themselves of all the valuable powers of the government, and inevitably reduce the people to a state of slavery, unless measures of reform are adopted before these despotisms are too firmly established to be overthrown.

By adopting the amendments to our constitutions indicated in this chapter, and inaugurating the organization of our legislatures, State and federal, to be presented in another work hereafter, the people will become in reality the only source of political power in the republic, under wise, harmonious, and just systems of laws, and a full representation of all individual citizens, property owners, and scholars from townships, villages, cities, and counties, in their primary capacities. This power they will exercise in three distinct houses of representation for the State and federal governments, the members whereof should be elected in the States by three distinct bodies of voters,—1st, the individual electors, comprising all citizens, who elect the members of the house of representatives; 2d, all the property-holders, who elect the members of the property house; and 3d, all the educated persons in the State, who elect the members of the academical house. These three houses will fully represent the people, the wealth, and the knowledge in the republic; the only powers that, harmoniously acting together, can successfully govern free states under federative systems of government.

The other great problem, how the rights of each State in a federative system like ours, and the proper supremacy of the federal government, can be secured so as to administer the laws and the governments for the common good, without tending towards centralization or disintegration, will also be examined in another work to be published hereafter.

II.

The main purpose of this work is to show the defects in the administration of our present systems of government, and to suggest remedies therefor. The most remarkable instances of maladministration in our federal affairs have occurred during the last ten years, which I propose to notice by way of illustration.

The passage of an act of Congress in 1863, for the creation of the national banks, was directly in conflict with the general principles above given as those that should govern the management of the national finances.

In 1861 the government issued sixty million dollars Treasury demand notes, receivable for duties, so that they were equivalent to coin in the New York market. During the year following about two hundred million dollars in legal-tender notes were issued, receivable for all debts except duties. Notwithstanding the ridiculous inconsistency of making these legal tenders inferior to coin, and inviting, as it were, coin gambling and a decline in the value of the legal-tender currency, no serious depreciation of it occurred until the issue of large amounts of federal bonds and the passage of the national bank act, in the spring of 1863, to increase the federal currency. This currency was to be issued by the government upon the basis of federal bonds deposited in the Treasury, to secure redemption in legal tenders. There was no valid reason for adopting this scheme to increase the circulation. The natural and reasonable course would have been to issue more legal-tender notes if they were needed.

The national bank expedient was infinitely worse in its effect upon our finances than a direct issue of one thousand million dollars of legal-tender notes would have been, for how could any sane man have supposed that national bank-notes issued by the Treasury upon federal bonds were better secured than legal-tender notes? This national bank issue was based upon the same national security, but it was not a legal tender for debts, and was redeemable in legal-tender notes, which made it an inferior currency. The whole commercial world regarded this scheme as a mere trick to bolster up the national bonds, and the immediate effect was greatly to injure and impair the public credit.

It is marvelous how any honest man could have proposed the passage of the national bank act to sustain the public credit, when by its terms the government agreed to pay such banks, when organized, twenty million dollars in coin per year for lending three hundred and thirty-three and one-third million dollars of second-class governmental currency to the people at the highest rate of interest for their own profit. No spendthrift heir ever sold his inheritance at more ruinous rates. Valuing the twenty million dollars in gold paid those banks as a bonus at the currency value in June, 1863, and estimating the interest thereon, compounded up to June, 1873, the banks would have realized a profit out of the bonus alone of nearly double their total circulation, and upon the circulation itself a further profit, estimated at nearly one thousand million of dollars.

These enormous amounts of money would have been saved to the people if the United States had issued the three hundred and thirty-three and one-third million dollars in legal-tender notes to meet war expenses in 1863, instead of chartering national banks to accomplish the same object in an indirect way, whereby the national credit was directly injured just in proportion as that notorious scheme of financial folly was manifestly unprofitable to the government; and accordingly it required, in July, 1864, about two hundred and seventy-five dollars in currency to buy one hundred dollars in gold.

The creation of these great money-monopolies, with their extravagant largesses from the government, emboldened shrewd and grasping speculators to demand and obtain from Congress, soon afterwards, inestimably valuable railway charters for roads to the Pacific coast, and vast grants of public lands, for the private emolument of a few favored stockholders.

These two schemes for using the sovereign powers of Congress for private profit are the most gigantic in their results of any recorded in history. The stockholders and managers of those corporations have probably realized in money and in lands enormous values, estimated to be nearly equal in amount to the whole national debt.

III.

There are other defects in the laws for the administration of our State and national governments which seriously impair the public intercommunication of our citizens, that should be remedied at once.

We require a State and national police and registration system that shall be effective for the protection of our lives and property, our political franchises, and our freedom from the improper interference of others. It is true that we have defective police systems in large cities, but they are wholly unable to accomplish the desired results. The coming and going of persons to and from the republic and all parts of it without any kind of registration, State or federal, is doubtless a very convenient arrangement for criminals, assassins, house-burners, and others, who desire to prey upon citizens and remain unknown; and it may appear to be an easy way for the citizens also, who will thus avoid the trouble of registration when they arrive at or depart from their residence or other place in the republic; but no plan of human construction can protect men in their "enjoyment of life, liberty, and the pursuit of happiness," unless the citizens are willing to submit to the slight inconveniences arising from a complete practical system of police and registration. This much-needed reform may seem irksome at first, but the annual increase of our terrible record of crime teaches us that if the criminal classes are not to rule us instead of being ruled by the law, we must render their existence and operations next to impossible by the inauguration of thorough police and registration systems, State and federal.

The numerous selfish combinations whereby railway and other monopolies unite to raise the rates of freight on produce and manufactured articles, so that farmers, miners, and manufacturers are unable to transport them to market with any profit, demand State and federal legislation for their suppression.

The whole body of our State and federal laws, civil, criminal, departmental, admiralty, military, naval, and inter-State national, should be codified, as well as the State and federal constitutions, whereupon the whole common-law system would be abolished, with its feudal features, monarchical foundations, and its more than eight hundred years of judicial discretion, oppression, and conflicting cases, the published reports whereof have become so voluminous that no one can master them, and but few lawyers afford to buy them. Thus has arisen, in the course of the administration of justice under the common-law system in England and in our country, the suggestive proverb, "There is a glorious uncertainty in the law." The "glory" can apply only to the lawyers and judges; the "uncertainty" is well known to the people, who continually suffer from it. There should not be any such inglorious "*uncertainty* in the law," for it is, of all science and knowledge, the most important to the citizen, who is presumed to know it, and yet may be convicted of felony, though ever so innocent, if he does not know it. But who can know the law if it is uncertain? And how unjust it is to require obedience to and enforcement of laws that are uncertain or unknown! and how terrible is the wrong when a court convicts a man of a crime for acts done that were not known at the time of their commission to be criminal! In abolishing the common law, the whole system of equity-law should be buried with it, being based upon the subterfuge that equity is only to be resorted to when there is no remedy at common law. Both these systems perpetually increase litigation by reason of the doubts arising in many cases as to which side of the court a party must apply to for relief or redress. There is no occasion in free states like ours for the use or practice of the vexing subtleties, mysteries, technicalities, and absurdities of the English systems of common and equity law, which are eminently adapted to perpetuate labor slavery, pauperism, monopolies, lordly oppressors, and the feudal monarchy and aristocracy of Great Britain, but not to promote the happiness of a free people. Moreover, the expenses of our law and equity system have become so onerous, by reason of its complications and absurdities, that a thorough codification and simplification of the laws and practice is imperatively demanded. The laws can be made plain and simple, and easily understood, if the principles are logically codified and plainly stated in good English, with all necessary forms of procedure, and made strictly applicable to the rights, duties, and obligations of all citizens, upon the common understanding and foundation of a perfect equality of rights, duties, and obligations.

We should place our whole system of federal taxation upon a rational and economical basis, by removing all duties and imports whatsoever, and levy only one tax to support the government, that shall be equitable and bear equally upon all citizens. The tariff system is so expensive, oppressive, unequal, and changeable, so fertile a source of all grades of crime and corruption, that as soon as our people become sufficiently instructed in their public duties and interests to establish a rational money system, they will abolish all tariffs and declare free trade to be the fundamental principle of our commercial intercommunication.

We should not permit Chinese labor slaves to be introduced into the republic and sold by their masters as they now are. We should not permit the exportation of felons, professional beggars, stolen children, assassins, and vagrants, the dregs and wrecks of despotisms from various European and Asiatic countries, to our republic, whereby their decaying society is relieved from the terrible influence of such wretches by shipping them here, to corrupt and destroy our own. These and other like evils would be readily remedied by the establishment of a State and federal police and registration system as herein proposed.

Every foreigner who comes to settle in this country, and applies for admission to citizenship, should be required to produce before the court clear proofs that he has abandoned his allegiance to all rulers, orders, castes, and directors whatsoever, of his former residence and country, and all other foreign countries, before he can demand the right of full naturalization; and if after the naturalization of any person it shall appear that he still acknowledges or yields any such allegiance as above, proceedings should be instituted to annul the certificate in any court having jurisdiction.

Many of the citizens of the United States are habitually avoiding the most important duties they owe to themselves and the state by neglecting to exercise their political functions at primary political meetings and as voters, thereby surrendering the elections to mere politicians, ward managers, ballot-box stuffers, and demagogues, and bringing the whole system of political management into contempt and ridicule. Laws cannot be enforced to compel citizens to vote, but if no better method be discovered to avert this growing evil, it might be provided by law that all citizens neglecting to exercise the elective franchise for two consecutive congressional elections, without a good excuse, should forfeit their right to hold any office of honor, trust, or profit in the State or federal government. Citizens should be admonished and warned that the exercise of the elective franchise, intelligently, without fear or favor, in a federative republic, is a sacred trust imposed upon them by their citizenship, and to be faithfully performed at all times, when the laws require elections for officers to administer the various functions of government. "The price of liberty is eternal vigilance." It is really a sort of petty treason to the state to exhibit carelessness and negligence in the performance of our public duties as citizens. This is the curse of all our American politics and laws; we are too careless and indifferent to devote time enough to examine into the seaworthiness of our ships of state and the manner of their navigation; we stay away from primary meetings, from the polls, from the courts of justice, and from the halls of legislation, as if we could avoid or remedy the maladministration of our public affairs by hiding from them in a spirit of cowardly indifference.

The establishment of polygamy in the Territory of Utah by the Mormon hierarchy, under a new theocratic despotism claimed to be formed for the lost tribes of Israel, and the influx of Asiatic populations into the Pacific States of the republic, with polygamy established under their customs, demand a remedy, which seems to be unattainable, unless the national Constitution is amended, so as to invest the federal government with power to enact laws to suppress this great evil. In that event national laws should be enacted establishing the monogamic system of marriage throughout the republic, and prohibiting polygamy in all its forms, thereby saving and preserving the female sex from the most abject slavery conceivable, which, during all recorded time, has always debased them body and soul under the dominion and curse of polygamy.

We should finally establish by law a system of State and national newspaper publications, to give the people official information of the most authentic character concerning the various administrations of our governments and branches of the public service, the new laws proposed to be made and the laws made, the governmental contracts, expenses, revenues, and losses, with a daily history of all the events of importance transpiring in the world, without any editorial comments. These papers to be furnished free of charge to all householders, heads of families, teachers, office-holders, army and navy officers, including subalterns of all grades, pensioners, ex-members of all descriptions of offices, and such other citizens as may be designated by law. Such newspapers to have the power to insert advertisements of all business, trade, commerce, etc., at such rates as to pay, if practicable, all the expenses of the publication.

In the first part of this work I have considered the measures a government based upon representative republican principles ought to adopt to secure each citizen in the fit and harmonious exercise of his functions as a physical member of the world of nature; then, in the second part, I have drawn the outlines of a system of schools, indicating my view of the measures necessary to aid and protect him in the proper exercise of his faculties as a member of the world of intelligence: in this third part I shall discuss the measures necessary to be adopted and enforced by the State and federal governments to secure all citizens in their commercial and public intercommunication, from all the hinderances and obstructions of all forms of monopoly or despotism.

No reforms demand speedier attention; and should some of them be deemed novel, they have all a pressing claim upon the study and attention of the statesman and the citizen. The preservation of the liberties of the people of these States depends, in my own opinion, upon a full, thorough, and comprehensive understanding and practical adoption of the plan proposed herein, or of a similar one in all of its main features.

MONEY.

CHAPTER I.

ORIGIN OF MONEY.

In the most primitive condition of man each individual furnished himself his own necessities. But as men begin to associate together and live in society this condition changes, and each one seeks to become a specific worker in some direction, while the chosen, rulers, teachers, etc., are engaged in no work at all directly productive of the necessities of life.

Thus there arose a system of barter or exchange for the workingmen, and for the officials a system of payment in kind, which gradually necessitated a system of tokens whereby to effect the interchange. There being yet no state organization sufficiently developed to make any token, no matter how intrinsically valueless, generally current by guaranteeing its permanent reception as such token for the value stated, the people naturally looked around for some substance which had great intrinsic value within small bulk. It was thus that gold and silver —sometimes also jewels and precious stones—became current; so that money, being virtually under no control of the state, except so far as its coining was concerned when gold and silver began to be coined for convenience, became a power over the state within the state, and a continually growing source of monopolies that, in point of fact, took away from the poorer class all their rights and privileges by a system of most cunningly exercised brokering and commercial despotism.

CHAPTER II.

INVENTION OF BANKING.

THUS money brokerage and exchange grew into a despotism more absolute than any other on earth, and has ever since retained this despotic power, which, wielded by men unscrupulous from the very nature of the case, has proved the greatest scourge of the human race. For gold and silver assumed a far greater significance than their own intrinsic value the moment these metals became the generally acknowledged medium of interchange among nations, since that acknowledgment made them virtually representatives of *all* the interchangeable commodities on earth, thereby increasing their value in proportion as this interchange increased. Thus with the growth of trade, commerce, and manufactures, the money-power assumed enormous proportions, and under the agency of shrewd men could be handled with terrific effect. The histories of Carthage and Tyre, of all the great "free" commercial cities of the Old World, of Phœnicia, Babylon, Egypt and Greece, are nothing but histories of the despotism of men and money corporations that knew how to use skillfully this potent agency; and in later times the same phenomena reappeared in the "free" cities of Northern Italy, Venice, Genoa, and Milan, where a few capitalists ruled with quite as severe a rod of tyranny as any emperor or king of history, nay, often even braving the whole power of emperors and kings.

But as Europe began to advance in civilization all the gold and silver attainable were not sufficient, even at the fabulous value to which they had been raised, to carry on the necessary business of this new-grown commercial world, and it was the necessity to provide for this state of things which led men's minds gradually to a proper notion of the true nature of money by inventing banking and exchanges. Through this invention the commercial world was supplied with a vast accession to the amount of money current in gold and silver, an accession which stimulated and made possible the extraordinary commercial activity of that period, and the adventurous undertakings to which it gave rise. The discovery of America, and the vast amounts of additional gold and silver or money thereby obtained, assisted still further to extend this prosperity in commerce, trade, and exchanges.

CHAPTER III.

CREATION OF STATE DEBTS.

BUT still the state refrained from interfering with this enormous power of the moneyed monopolies. Within the political states of Europe there were thus always two other despotisms besides that of the government itself: the hierarchical, and the despotism of money; and under the three the people were left little of their natural liberties and rights indeed. It seems strange that no state ever conceived the plan of taking that tremendous power of money out of the hands of the financiers by establishing a money of its own; but even to-day the old state of things continues, in a measure, as it has been shaped by circumstances and innumerable contradictory individual theories and efforts. George Law, it is true, tried to induce France to adopt some such policy of pure paper money; but the attempt was not thorough, and was, moreover, joined with other schemes for private speculation. In one way, however, the states of Europe did improve the example set by the men of money. These latter had increased their supply of currency by the banking system, using drafts and letters of credit as temporary representatives of money at different points in the world; the whole system depending, however, upon cons'ant renewal and extension, and hence constituting those drafts and letters of credit real money in all respects. The states now instead of issuing letters of credit began to issue bonds, and with the beginning of the Napoleonic wars this addition of money values flooded Europe in a wonderful way. For these state bonds are in reality also nothing but money, their improvement on the letters of credit or paper money being in the fact that they bear interest. This improvement is, however, a one-sided one altogether, being in favor of the capitalist and against the tax-payers of the state, and has been adopted only from supposed necessity, as a compromise, inducement and bribe given to the capitalist to recognize these bonds as money.

To exhibit the way in which money values have in this manner been added to the representative wealth of the world, let us consider the following table of the comparative debts in pounds sterling of twenty-six governments in 1862 and 1872:

	1862.	1872.	Increase.
Argentine Republic	£3,000,000	£17,500,000	£14,500,000
Austria	250,000,000	300,000,000	50,000,000
Belgium	26,200,000	30,000,000	3,800,000
Bolivia	....	2,000,000	2,000,000
Brazil	5,000,000	60,000,000	55,000,000
Chili	2,800,000	7,500,000	4,700,000
Costa Rica	....	3,400,000	3,400,000
Danubian Principalities	....	5,000,000	5,000,000
Denmark	11,000,000	12,800,000	1,800,000
Egypt	3,300,000	45,000,000	41,700,000
France	396,000,000	970,000,000	574,000,000
Germany	60,000,000	120,000,000	60,000,000
Guatemala	300,000	600,000	300,000
Honduras	....	5,000,000	5,000,000
Italy	100,000,000	275,000,000	175,000,000
Japan	....	1,000,000	1,000,000
Mexico	20,000,000	60,000,000	40,000,000

	1862.	1872.	Increase.
Paraguay	....	3,000,000	3,000,000
Peru	5,500,000	37,000,000	31,500,000
Portugal	33,000,000	65,000,000	32,000,000
Russia	230,000,000	350,000,000	120,000,000
Spain	150,000,000	306,000,000	156,000,000
Sweden	3,000,000	6,000,000	3,000,000
Turkey	23,000,000	130,000,000	107,000,000
United States	75,000,000	470,000,000	395,000,000
Uruguay	4,000,000	6,000,000	2,000,000
Venezuela	5,000,000	8,000,000	3,000,000
Total	£1,493,100,000	£3,375,800,000	£1,882,700,000

A very noticeable fact in this list is, that the younger states of the world have so quickly perceived the advantages of this system of creating money credits, and followed so successfully in the tracks of their elders of European descent. The Argentine Republic increases her money credits in ten years from $15,000,000 to $87,000,000, Bolivia from a mere nominal amount to $10,000,000, Brazil from $25,000,000 to $300,000,000, and Egypt from $16,500,000 to $225,000,000.

All in all, it appears from the above table that, within ten years, twenty-six governments of the world have increased the amount of money bonds circulating, to the extent of $9,413,000,000; England meanwhile remaining stationary in her issue, and Holland alone reducing her debt or outstanding funds some $35,000,000.

This fact and this alone explains the marvelous increase in the wealth of almost all nations of the world. The wealth of the United States, for instance, which was about seven thousand million dollars in 1850, rose to sixteen thousand millions in 1860, then in the next decade, amidst a war which destroyed nine thousand million dollars of property, it rose to the enormous sum of thirty thousand million of dollars, and could never have assumed these vast proportions, had not the issue of paper money and bonds furnished the necessary circulating medium. For money credits can be quite as readily transferred from one place to another in the shape of bonds as in the shape of notes, and hence every bond serves as a means of exchange between the various cities of the country, and in another way too between this country and foreign countries. The issue of bonds by any state in the world in this way increases by so much the circulation of world-money, and contributes to the wealth of all nations using them as exchange.

If Great Britain has accumulated more wealth since the beginning of this century than she had during all the eighteen hundred years previous, the explanation can be seen in the above table of debts; the benefit of which Great Britain has enjoyed more than other nations in proportion as she has been the chief negotiator of most of them, and has been able to use successfully, during all the Napoleonic wars, the national currency of the Bank of England during the long suspension of specie payments occasioned by those wars. This national money has given her a monetary supremacy over all the nations of the world.

Again, the remarkable prosperity which all Europe, and particularly France, enjoyed since the close of the frightful Franco-German war, when every one expected France would be as financially ruined as she was politically, is properly understood only by looking upon the issues of the five milliard loan as so much circulating wealth added in the short space of two years to the money of Western Europe.

Nothing is, therefore, more true than the seeming financial paradox that the contracting of debts increases the circulating exchange-wealth of the world ; and this paradox must necessarily remain true until all nations of the world have swept away their debts by substituting paper money in their place, and issuing enough of it for the requirements of their states. The paradox will then cease to be one by being shaped into its rational formula, that the issue of the necessary amount of money needed by a state is not in the nature of a debt, but the prerogative inherent in the sovereignty of the state, to issue the representation of the entire wealth of the state, in a circulating medium.

Nothing else, moreover, explains the extraordinary fact, that the discovery of gold in California and Australia did not produce a steady decline in the price of gold, and that the average price of wheat is to-day nearly the same as it was in 1850, when it was about one dollar. What a great outcry was then raised by M. Michel Chevalier, of France, and De Quincey, in England, about the ruin impending over the world by reason of the fall in the price of gold it was supposed would necessarily follow those discoveries. If gold had then been and had continued to be the only world-money, their prophecies might have been in part fulfilled. But the fact is that gold had ceased to be the only world-money for a long time, and that the infinitely greater part of world-money was even then already made of paper.

If the value of gold has since fluctuated so vastly in our own country, the reason is to be found mainly in the lack of energy on the part of our government, that dared not proclaim its right to be the only money-making power for its own needs, and partly in a spirit of speculation or gambling that never seriously affected the real value of paper money. For all commodities and labor of the United States are very little changed in price now, that gold is $1.15, from the time when gold was $2.15.

To demonstrate in a most telling manner that the issuing of bonds and the system of banking is to all intents and purposes an increasing of the real money of the world, I may mention the fact that Sir John Lubbock in analyzing the nineteen millions of the receipts of the banking-house of Messrs. Robarts & Co., of London, discovered that only three per cent. of those receipts were in cash,—that is, in gold or bank-notes,—and the ninety-seven per cent. were checks, drafts, and other means of exchange. That is to say, Messrs. Robarts & Co., with cash receipts of only five hundred and seventy thousand pounds, were enabled to furnish their customers by the artificial means of bank-accounts, etc., means and money to conduct nineteen million pounds' worth of business. Of course the customers paid Messrs. Robarts & Co. heavy discounts, etc., for being the intermediating agency in this transfer of credits and balances; but, under such a system of governmental money as I have here developed, those discounts could be reduced to a mere trifle of actual expense; and with even a smaller percentage of actual so-called cash on hand, our government could safely undertake and guarantee the transfer of all the milliards of dollars per annum needed by the business, commerce, and the farming interests of our country.

CHAPTER IV.

THE CURSE OF INTEREST.

WHILE in so far the issue of these bonds has been a blessing to the people by furnishing them the needed means of exchange of values, in another way it has been a curse, and as curses all grow with age, so the weight of this curse is to be felt only in the future in all its crushing power. This curse is the interest attached to the bonds, the inevitable coupon, for which the state that issues the bond gets nothing, and which, with its accumulating force of compound interest, must necessarily ruin every state ultimately, or force it into bankruptcy.

This curse is the result of cowardice; the state being afraid to assume the same power which some few banking-houses, not within one million times so wealthy as the state, were superstitiously supposed to possess, of converting their issues of paper into money, which is the real philosopher's stone. Like all other superstitions this one will have to be swept away, so as to relieve labor of the burdens these money-monopolies impose upon it.

The absurd fact is, that a sovereign state, finding say one hundred million more of dollars necessary for its circulation, did not dare to meet the exigency by simply making the amount of money needed, but in a roundabout sort of way issued some paper money, called bonds, and going to capitalists, say one or two large bankers, like the Rothschilds, or Jay Cooke & Co., begged them to be pleased to recognize this paper money as good current money; which these bankers agreed to do upon payment of a large immediate discount and a continuous future semi-annuity, called interest, which is the tribute paid these money-kings.

The state having agreed to the terms of this contract, the capitalists put the profits into their pockets, and told the people of the state that those paper-moneys or bonds were good current money, and thus, having made manifest their supreme power over their own sovereign state, looked around for some other power to subdue in the same manner, by compelling it to pay interest tribute.

It is apparent that for a whole people constituting a state to thus put such an immense monopoly into the hands of a few capitalists, either at home or abroad, is ruinous to their liberties and welfare, and that the accumulation of interest compounded in such manner must eventually swallow up the whole property and values of the state. Why should these capitalists have the power to say what is to be money? Why should not the people themselves in their organic law decide upon this matter, and agree among themselves what they all intend to receive as money, thus all pledging to each one the security of the money and the permanency of its value forever? The only objection made is this: that so long as each state of the world is an absolutely separate organization, the paper money of one state can never become the legal currency of any other state, and that gold and silver must therefore always remain the only possible world-money. To what extent this objection is valid, and how it is to be overcome, will be considered hereafter.

There is, however, still another and even more disastrous view to be taken of this issuing of interest-bearing bonds by a state. It is virtually the mortgaging by the state as a political body of all the rights, liberties, wealth, and franchises of its citizens to foreign bondholders; and to what extent this can be carried was very effectively shown in the case of Mexico, when the foreign bondholders, with their claims upon the state of over eighty-three millions of dollars, succeeded in inducing their European governments to impose a foreign emperor upon the Mexican people, plunging them into those fatal wars that were to end in the tragic death of Maximilian.

No state government should have the power to

sell its citizens into possible foreign slavery, thus laying a mine under the political fabric that may at any moment shatter it into fragments. The issue of bonds bearing interest is the exercise of such power. It puts shackles on a nation even more effectually than a mortgage does on the individual who hypothecates his farm.

The issue of paper money, on the contrary, has no such enslaving power. It does not pretend to be convertible into gold, silver, copper, lead, wheat, cotton, or other articles of merchandise, but is a legal tender, and the only legal tender, in the state that issues it. If an international clearing-house be established, the failure of any state at any time to make good its balance in the values agreed upon between the several nations composing the clearing-house would not result in war, but simply in the expulsion of such nation from the clearing-house, thereby virtually excluding it from all foreign trade and commerce until it restored its credit by proper measures.

Still more: the issue of paper money by any federation of states would constitute the strongest bond of union for its citizens. The most vital interests of every one would be enlisted in maintaining the government and to prevent disintegration. Our late civil war would have been impossible if a national paper currency had made the fortune and prosperity of every citizen dependent upon the maintenance of the common government and federation.

And in a similar way the further extension of such a system of money to all the civilized nations of the earth, and the establishment by them of an international clearing-house, would unite all those different states together by the closest possible tie, and contribute more than any other measure to prevent the occurrence of war.

CHAPTER V.

THE TRUE NATURE OF MONEY.

THE true theory of money is therefore this: Money is a necessary means of intercommunication between all the citizens of a state. To leave the control of such intercommunication to the freaks of chance, as to how much gold and silver may be found or not, or to put it within the power of any body of men conspiring together for such control, is in the latter case to endanger the liberties of all citizens, and in the former to leave their welfare exposed to the mercy of the elements of nature. Hence it becomes the duty of the state to take the matter altogether and exclusively under its own control, to determine what shall be money, and to provide it at all times in sufficient quantities to meet the necessities of the people, increasing the quantity in proportion as the growth of the trade, commerce, and products of the state require it. In this one proposition lies concealed the philosopher's stone ages have exerted their best efforts to discover.

The question is, how much money should be issued? The whole amount of money circulating in a state represents the whole interchangeable commodities within the state; hence it is in one way altogether the same how much or how little money the first issue is, that issue gaining its standard of value not from its convertibility into coin, but from its convertibility into the purchasable products of the state. But as gold and silver with their divisions into dollars and cents have once been adopted as a standard of value, it is as well to retain that standard; and hence a well-organized state should issue in tokens of the least possible intrinsic value—say paper-tokens—such an amount of dollars and cents as would represent at the adopted standard all the interchangeable commodities of the state; and increase this sum in proportion to the increase of the commerce, manufactures, and other enterprises and riches of the state, so that money should never be scarce, but elastically adopt itself to every change and circumstance.

The amount needed at first for circulation as well as the successive additions required can be determined with ease by a proper system of statistics, which for that purpose ought to be gathered at least once in each year, and can be for many years admirably regulated by calling in the outstanding interest-bearing bonds. Thus the people will be at the same time supplied with money sufficient to meet their wants and circumstances, as they ought to be furnished, since money is as necessary to them as the air they breathe, and must be furnished them in larger proportions as they grow and require more for their daily use, and relieved of a burdensome tax called interest, which in its usual compound character is ultimately certain to impoverish the state.

In other words, money must be made a blessing to the people, and not remain the means whereby a few place shackles on the many, and establish the most oppressive and crushing of all despotisms; which always falls with double force upon the laborers and producers in the state.

CHAPTER VI.

HISTORY OF OUR PAPER MONEY.

I.

IN the year of the Declaration of Independence of the United States, the Continental Congress, having no control of sufficient gold and silver to carry on the revolutionary war, was forced by that great exigency to establish a paper currency, and authorize the issue of such money as the only available means for exchanging values and prosecuting the conflict with Great Britain to a successful issue; but it had no clear comprehension of the sovereign right of the new republic to create a national money of its own. During the year 1776 twenty million dollars were issued, and before the close of the war more than three hundred and fifty-seven million dollars of continental currency was in circulation in the United States.

While the colonists were battling for their right to a free representative government against the despotism of the British Parliament, they did not seem to be aware of the fact that an equally dangerous money-despotism, controlled and wielded with great skill by their adversary, could be counterbalanced only by a national financial system of their own creation. To a certain extent this was accomplished by the plan adopted; but if that Congress had made its currency, to the exclusion of all other money, a legal tender for all demands, secured, as it would have been, by the wealth and resources of the nation, even then so richly endowed, a rational money system would have been established by the new republic, facilitating the triumph of its arms, compensating it for the great losses and expenses of the war, and at the same time breaking the shackles of the money-despotisms of the Old World in our republic, which to this day continue to oppress and embarrass our people.

The continental money was created merely as a temporary war measure, necessary to insure success to our arms in that memorable conflict; but as soon as the crisis was over, it was repudiated in bad faith, to the ruin of many patriotic soldiers and citizens, and the injury of our national credit and financial standing among nations. If that currency had been made a legal tender when issued, the total amount of the issues would not have been one-fourth of the amount repudiated in 1782–83, and would have greatly added to the prosperity of the people of the States, by giving them a universal national money-medium of intercommunication to develop their inexhaustible resources, to unfold to full activity all the producing, manufacturing, trading, and commercial industries of the people, and to defend them against and emancipate them from all foreign as well as domestic monetary monopolies. After that repudiation, great financial distress ensued, paralyzing all kinds of business, for the want of money to carry it on, until the year 1791, when the establishment of a United States bank by Congress relieved in a great degree the previous money-pressure.

The charter of that bank expired in 1811, and no other money-tokens remaining but gold and silver, wholly insufficient in quantity to furnish a circulating medium for the increasing business and commerce of the people, another period of suffering for the want of money ensued, and the war of 1812, with Great Britain, so increased it, that a second United States bank of issue was chartered for twenty years, in 1816, which again temporarily relieved and restored the business activity of the people.

II.

At length the States of the republic began to charter banks with power to issue paper money, in violation of the spirit of the Constitution; although the federal Supreme Court, under the pressure of an apparent public necessity, held their charters to be valid. The paper-money issues of the federal and State banks furnished a large addition to the circulation and exchanges; but different kinds of money were thus introduced, in addition to coin, and the almost universal depreciation of the value of many of the State bills at any considerable distance from the place of their issue and redemption injuriously affected business and commerce, by subjecting such bank-notes to brokerage discounts, and thereby forcing the banks into a continual warfare with each other, to compel coin redemptions for the protection of their several issues.

This kept alive and flourishing the coin-money system, and finally created a conflict between the federal banks and State banks, that culminated in 1833, when President Jackson, espousing the cause of the State banks, compelled the government moneys to be removed from the United States Bank to certain State banks, which became the depositaries of the public moneys and the authorized agents of the Treasury. The opposition of the President and the Democratic party, and the removal of the deposits, caused the downfall of the federal bank, and the national credit and moneys passed to the State banks that were known as "pet banks."

III.

Then arose an era of irresponsible, illegal State banking, controlled exclusively by private corporations, for their own profit, resulting in enormous issues of paper money, causing an extravagant inflation of the currency and increasing speculative manias, to such an extent that nearly all those banks suspended in 1837, with an irredeemable currency flooding the country. The universal distress and prostration of all business and trade was such that Congress passed acts, in 1837, 1838, and 1839, for the issue of Treasury notes to the amount of ten million dollars in each of those years, for the relief of the people,. by furnishing them a national money amply secured by the credit and vast resources of the republic.

IV.

These laws gave some temporary relief to the extraordinary stringency of the money market, but the government did not yet perceive the true remedy for financial revulsions to be a national currency, and these wise acts were repealed in 1841, and Congress in the same year deemed it necessary to pass a national bankrupt act.

The State banks that did not forfeit their charters or discontinue their business one after another resumed specie payments, and the working of the monetary system under their management, from 1843 to 1861, illustrated the ruinous results arising from the delegation to States or corporations of the sovereign power of making money or issuing notes to form a circulating medium for the people of the United States.

The frequent recurrence of panics during that period proved this by demonstrating the fallacy of keeping up a permanent circulation of paper money, issued by divers State banks, that was always to be redeemable in specie on demand. The mutual jealousy of such banks will ultimately reduce the circulation to the coin on hand, and a great scarcity of money will ensue; or if the issues greatly exceed the specie in their vaults, and a demand for gold arises, as in 1857, the banks so organized must suspend specie payments, to the ruin and distress of all persons depending upon their circulation for the transaction of business.

V.

At the breaking out of our civil war in 1861, the federal government had no paper money outstanding, and gold and silver were its only recognized standard of value. It immediately became apparent that sums of money immensely beyond the sum of all the gold and silver on hand would be needed, to supply the sinews of war, and the stringency seemed all the greater in that the effects of the monetary crisis of 1857–58 had not yet passed away. The State banks had already proved wholly inefficient for managing the monetary affairs of the nation in time of peace, even with the assistance of the Sub-treasury, organized in 1846; and no other course remained than the organization of a money system independent of coin, and in July, 1861, the issue of sixty million dollars of demand notes, receivable for duties and imposts, was authorized by Congress.

But the government, instead of continuing the money-policy thus inaugurated and making all its issues a legal tender for all debts thereafter contracted, changed the issue, from 1862 to 1864, to legal-tender notes, receivable for all debts except duties and imposts. Four hundred million dollars of this currency were issued during that period, and to make it the supreme paper money of the country, a heavy tax was levied upon the circulation of the State banks, which were thereby virtually suppressed.

Thus three kinds of money were established: the demand notes, the legal-tender notes, and gold and silver,—placing a premium on the coin, over which the government had no control. The legal-tender currency issue was too small, and for some unaccountable reason Congress would not authorize the issue of more currency, and hence was forced to create a fourth kind of money, in the form of bonds of the United States, bearing heavy interest payable in coin,—although the principal of these bonds, known as 5-20's, was generally understood to be payable in legal-tender currency,—and caused them to be sold at a ruinous discount for gold, which Congress had greatly enhanced in price by requiring all duties to be paid to the agents of the Treasury in specie, thus directly depreciating the legal-tender notes by refusing to receive them for duties payable to the government.

The issue of these interest-bearing bonds during the war forced the government into the market to sell its own securities for its own legal-tender notes or for gold, and to do this it was deemed necessary to employ bankers and brokers, pay heavy commissions, and contract immense future obligations in the way of interest, in order that some banking-houses, with not a millionth part of its wealth and resources, might indorse its bonds and undertake their negotiation. Thus this wealthy and powerful government, by an unpardonable financial blunder, placed its finances at the mercy of foreign and domestic money-monopolies; nay, sacrificed the wealth and prosperity of future generations, by unnecessarily incurring an interest debt which already demands a most oppressive rate of taxation and duties to meet it.

VI.

The true policy, and the one suggested to the Secretary of the Treasury at the breaking out of the war, was to recommend to Congress the passage of a law for the creation of a national money, by the issue of legal-tender Treasury notes, receivable for all debts, demands and duties, to the exclusion of all other money, thereby rendering gold and silver mere articles of commerce, like copper, lead, iron and other products for import or export.

If this proposed policy had been approved by the Secretary of the Treasury, or adopted by Congress without his recommendation, the war expenses would have been greatly diminished, and at the restoration of peace there would have been no national bonded war debt and no national taxes, and the people would have had a reliable national money for general circulation, to the exclusion of all other money, and better suited for business, commercial, and governmental purposes than any other money in the world.

Instead of adopting this economical and statesmanlike policy to meet the public exigency, many vacillating, speculative, and unwise schemes were proposed by the Treasury, adopted by Congress, and abandoned alternately, until the bond credit of the United States, in 1864, sank below that of the Confederate States about twenty per cent. in the London money market. This was the plain result of our own inconsistent, suicidal financial schemes, as will clearly appear from a brief review of them.

The issue of the demand notes first issued was followed by an issue of common legal-tender notes issued in lieu of them, then coin interest-bearing 5-20 bonds, 7-30 interest-bearing bonds, Treasury three-year notes, three per cent. certificates, more 5-20 bonds and gold certificates, until about two thousand million dollars 5-20 bonds had been issued.

In fact, the main purpose of the financial administration of our affairs during the whole progress of the war seemed to be to create an enormous national debt, bearing a high rate of interest, and entailing upon the people ruinous taxes, tariffs, and other burdens.

But worse than all these extravagant and inconsistent measures, the government, finding that the people needed more currency for ready interchange, instead of issuing legal-tender notes in proportion as they were needed, created, in 1863, one of the most powerful monopolies in the world, by the National Bank Act, and transferred to the money corporations to be organized thereunder the national sovereign power of making United States national bank-notes, paying them, moreover, virtually an annuity of six per cent. in coin to accept this most valuable franchise.

In 1869 there were sixteen hundred and twenty of these national banks, with a circulation of two hundred and ninety-nine million seven hundred and eighty-nine thousand eight hundred and ninety-five dollars, secured by United States 5-20 bonds for three hundred and forty-two million four hundred and seventy-five thousand six hundred dollars, deposited by them in the Treasury to secure their several circulations, issued upon such bonds, the redemption of which in legal-tender notes was guaranteed by the United States. That is, the government paid those sixteen hundred and twenty banks an interest bonus of six per cent. in coin a year on three hundred and forty-two million four hundred and seventy-five thousand six hundred dollars of United States bonds, to accept the privilege of issuing three hundred million dollars of such currency so issued to them, and loaning them out at the highest rates of interest.

This ruinous scheme of finance, invented, it is said, in the Treasury, to aid the federal government, is about equivalent to a loan of money by Mr. Prodigal to Mr. Shylock for twenty years, on a special agreement that the lender should pay the borrower six per cent. yearly interest in coin for accepting the money so loaned, and assuming the trouble of lending it, at the highest rate of usury possible, for his own profit!

But in order to rivet these chains of debt and interest more firmly upon the necks of the people, so that no future Congress could remove them, it was necessary for the bondholders, brokering speculators, and the national bank stockholders to procure the passage of a law declaring the 5-20 currency bonds to be redeemable only in coin; and to prevent the repeal of such an unjust law, another enactment was required, authorizing the issue of new bonds, with special contracts inserted therein, binding the government to pay the principal and interest in coin, whereby, on the sale of the new bonds for gold, the proceeds would be used for the redemption of the 5-20 currency bonds in coin.

To accomplish this purpose, Congress, on the 18th of March, 1869, passed a joint resolution, pledging the faith of the nation to redeem the 5-20 bonds in gold; and on the 14th of July, 1870, another act, authorizing the issue of new gold bonds with gold coupons, to be sold for the redemption of the 5-20 currency bonds at par.

About two thousand million dollars of 5-20 currency bonds were thus changed into coin bonds by the act of 1869, the burdens of it falling with crushing force upon the tax-payers and producers of the present and future generations of our own people. These 5-20 bonds had most of them been purchased at an average coin price of about fifty cents on the dollar. By this inexcusable legislation of Congress the national debt and all secured debts of individuals, contracted for currency during the war, were in reality doubled, for the sole benefit of usurers, bondholders, and monopolists, and a new obligation was created for the American people, which it is impossible to fulfill. There is not half gold enough to be had anywhere to pay off the 5-20 bonds. It is a physical impossibility, and, by the resolution assuming to pay it in coin, Congress virtually forced upon the nation a gigantic short sale of two thousand million dollars in gold for two thousand million dollars in 5-20 bonds that had already been sold for currency prices and were then outstanding, to be redeemed in legal tenders.

It was a bold, treasonable cornering of the nation in the interest of the bondholders; and, injurious as its consequences have already been in producing universal financial distress and numerous bankruptcies, the far more threatening calamities of national insolvency and revolution that it holds out for the future can be avoided only by the repeal of the acts of 1869–70, and the passage of an act prohibiting the further sale of new gold bonds, and requiring the redemption of all the remaining 5-20 currency bonds in legal-tender notes to be issued for that purpose, as was the original intention and understanding.

VII.

But even these miserably inconsistent financial measures of issuing several different kinds of Treasury notes, bonds, and national bank-notes demonstrated in a general way the wisdom of making a national money controllable by the government. An era of prosperity for the United States began, and continued from 1863 to 1869–70, that made us almost forget the expenses and ravages of a gigantic civil war. Commerce, agriculture, and manufactures multiplied in wonderful proportions, and great public improvements of all kinds increased rapidly on every side; and this national prosperity would in all probability have been permanent if the acts of 1869–70 had not been passed, and a policy had not been adopted by the Treasury subjecting the established national currency to a ruinous conflict with the old coin despotism, supporting and supported by the money-monopolies that now rule the nation with a rod of iron.

VIII.

Before these incorporated despotisms the federal Congress, many of the State legislatures, and great numbers of the people bowed down in submissive adoration, like the idolatrous Hebrews in their worship of the golden calf at Mount Sinai; and now, since these powers are supposed to have attained absolute supremacy, the redemption of the 5-20 bonds in coin and the sale of the new gold bonds are urged with such eager haste by the Treasury that financial ruin stares our merchants and manufacturers in the face, and the bankrupt courts are overrun with applications. To complete our financial ruin we need but one more suicidal act of Congress, providing for the resumption of specie payments, which would bring the fatal conflict between the legal-tender currency system of the country and the old coin despotism to a close by destroying our national money, and inevitably force the nation and the people into bankruptcy, repudiation, or revolution.

Happily it is now wholly impracticable to return to a coin basis, and if it were possible, such a money famine would be produced as never has been known in history. It would unsettle all values, embarrass all trade, destroy all confidence and all credit. The only reasonable course to pursue, therefore, is to issue legal-tender demand notes in sufficient quantity to redeem all the outstanding 5-20 bonds at par, and let Congress declare such bonds to be redeemable in that currency; these legal-tender notes to be declared, moreover, the only national money receivable for property, debts, and *duties* in the United States. This would give us a far better money system than we have now or ever have had; it would restore trade, commerce, and all industries to a sound and prosperous condition, and at the same time prevent the monopolizing money corporations of the country from unjustly taxing the people in the way of interest for the use of money that really belongs to the government.

CHAPTER VII.

FOREIGN EXCHANGES AND AN INTERNATIONAL CLEARING HOUSE.

THE one objection raised against such irredeemable paper money is, that it would check all foreign commerce, since foreign countries would not recognize it.

To this objection I reply,—1st. That the citizens of foreign countries do recognize our paper money. They bought and buy our bonds, knowing that with these bonds they could buy any purchasable commodity in the United States, and would not have bought them had they not known and believed this. The outrageous discount we paid them for taking them was simply a swindle imposed on our own people by ourselves. 2d. The interchange between our markets and those of foreign countries is regulated in the main by the imports and exports, by exchange from other countries, etc. Silver is even at this day already almost altogether an article of merchandise, and gold will very soon be one also if governments exercise their power to make paper money and exchange. With only one kind of money in the state, the price of those articles of merchandise, gold and silver, will regulate itself just as that of all other articles of merchandise does. The European capitalist will, for instance, just as soon hoard one thousand dollars of United States paper money as one thousand dollars' worth of gold, when he knows for a certainty that it will buy him the same amount of wheat, or lands, or cotton; and the chances of a fall or rise in the price of gold he will take just as readily as he takes the chances of the rise or fall in other products.

In the course of time it will, no doubt, be feasible to arrange treaties with all civilized foreign countries regulating the value and standard of money, and thereby to allay altogether this spectre of foreign exchange, under pretext of which the people are imposed upon in every direction by money-monopolies. The superstitious notions concerning the god of Mammon, as represented by gold and silver, must be swept away, even like all other superstitions handed down to us by preceding generations.

To state this feasibility in the concisest way, it is quite as practicable to establish an international clearing-house, as it has been found practicable to establish clearing-houses in every large city. In this international clearing-house the paper moneys or drafts of each separate state in the world would be sent for exchange, as such exchange may be wanted, and rules could easily be arranged between the several nations composing this international clearing-house, concerning the way in which the balances should be settled or adjusted, and the international code and judicial department for the administration of international justice would aid the clearing-house in effecting these measures.

Situated as our country is, in the most favorable

geographical position, between the two great oceans of the world, the developed civilization of Europe on the east, and the wealth of Asia on the west, connected already with the one continent by several lines of telegraphic cable, and undoubtedly soon to be connected in like manner with the East Indies, China, and Japan, exhibiting a wealth many million times in excess of our outstanding circulation, and a productiveness in all articles of commerce which under the exercise of judicious economy, is amply sufficient to balance our imports by our exports, and having the capacity of establishing a commercial marine that would control the commerce of the two oceans, no other nation is so able and competent to introduce the purely rational system of money herein developed, and be the first to reap its incalculable blessings.

Every citizen is most intimately concerned in aiding the government to establish and perfect this monetary system, and thereby to strike the shackles that have so long fettered us, off our arms, and to keep the generations that shall succeed us free from them. The conflicts between capital and labor that harass us, the exorbitant rates of interest, the sudden changes of value that plunge so many from wealth into poverty, and the spread of pauperism, which looms up threateningly for the future, all find their permanent remedy only in the establishment of a system of money that shall be under the control of the government, instead of self-interested monopolies, that are gradually absorbing the wealth and liberties of the people.

PUBLIC HIGHWAYS.

CHAPTER I.

THE NATURE OF HIGHWAYS.

THE state guarantees to each citizen full protection in the harmonious and fit enjoyment of all the faculties of his mind and body. In order to be able to make good this guarantee the state must be able to have access to all citizens, and they with each other and with the state. The right of the state to have such access constitutes its right and duty to lay out public highways and regulate the intercourse thereby established between its citizens. The state must, moreover, have the right of the speediest access to its citizens, for how could the state guarantee protection to each citizen if other citizens had speedier access to him? If the state had control only over common roads, while criminally aggressive citizens had control over railways, where would be the sovereign power?

Furthermore: since in a well-regulated state each citizen has his specific vocation, and thus is dependent upon being able to have transmitted to him the productions of all other vocations which he stands in need of, the state must be in a position to govern all such transmission, and hence must have full control over all means of transmission or communication, of which there are at present three: those of postal, those of telegraphic, and those of commercial intercommunication. For in no other way could the state guarantee to each citizen his right to all the products of others, which are purchasable, and which he by his labors in his vocation is able to purchase.

CHAPTER II.

THE MAIL AND THE TELEGRAPH.

For some inscrutable reason the state has hitherto conceived it to be the duty of government to take control of only one species of intercommunication, that of letters. For this reason government has established a post-office department, by means of which all its citizens are guaranteed the right of correspondence by written letter. At the same time this department has selected one species of merchandise for governmental transmission, that of printed matter, though only in a limited extent. It is hard to say why, with the invention of the telegraph as a quicker mode of communication than that by letter, government did not at once take control of it. The same principle underlies the telegraph as the mail: that it is the duty of the state to secure to each citizen sure communication with every other citizen in the quickest possible manner. To leave this matter to private corporations is unsafe and leads to the establishment of monopolies, that are a constant oppression of the people and a permanent danger to the state itself.

In a well-organized government, therefore, the state itself will take possession of all lines of telegraph, and operate them exclusively for the benefit of the people; and submarine lines of telegraph connecting foreign states across oceans, gulfs, lakes, and bays, should be put under the control of the two states thus connected, so that neither the people nor the government of those states may be dependent upon, and at the mercy of, private monopolies.

It is no easy task to make men realize the danger threatening from such an extraordinary monopoly as the telegraph system has grown to be in our country. Sure of the permanence of our republican institutions, we allow these agencies of tyranny to grow up without check or hinderance, and to increase their power by consuming the lesser attempts at rivalry and competition in the simplest manner, that is to say, by buying them out. All European states, one after another, have found it necessary to take control of the telegraph, and in every case the result has been of the greatest advantage and profit to the people. Great Britain was the last one to take the control of the telegraph from private monopolies and exercise it solely for the advantage of the state at large; and while under corporate management the telegraphic communications had increased only from six millions in 1860 to eight millions in 1868, which is an average annual increase of only fifteen per cent., under the management of the government the business steadily increased at an annual average of thirty-three per cent. This extraordinary result was mainly due to the fact that when the British government took charge of all the telegraph lines in 1870, it at once lowered the rates one-third.

Private corporations are always very slow in reducing rates. If the mail business had been put into the hands of private express companies the charges of postage would still be at rates now long since abolished. But the government, being interested in no dividend account, and making its calculations only on the basis of accommodating the greatest number of people, without any other expense than the mere accommodation costs, acts on an entirely different principle, and accordingly invites additional business by lowering rates. We all know what an immense increase of letter-writing followed the introduction of the present low rates of postage. Were government to take hold of the telegraph lines and reduce the rates as Great Britain has done, or Belgium, the business of the telegraph would doubtless quadruple in the course of two or three years. As it is, our rates of telegraphing are twice as high as the rates are in England, and three times as high as rates in Belgium; and the result has been, that while the increase in the number of messages sent in Great Britain since 1870 has been an average of thirty-three per cent. per annum, the increase in our country has been only sixteen per cent. The people have a right to the speediest and cheapest mode of intercommunication with each other, and it is the duty of the government to furnish it and guarantee its accuracy and certainty.

Still, it is not alone in this respect that the telegraph business needs the control of government. It not only hinders intercommunication under private management, but it has become one of the monopolies that virtually rule the country with despotic sway. Its growth into this power is a curious one, though the same phenomenon has been witnessed in every other country that first allowed private corporations to undertake enterprises that were peculiarly within the right and duty of the state to establish.

No sooner did the first telegraph between Washington and New York prove a success than all over the country occurred a general pole-raising and wire-stretching, wholly regardless of the immediate prospects of sufficient earnings to maintain the lines. In our usual style we discounted the future most liberally, organized small companies in the various villages of the land, and looked on composedly as one after the other broke up, the larger ones feeding on the smaller awhile, then themselves swallowed by the still larger ones, until only two were left to devour each other: the Western Union, with the main business of the country from New York to San Francisco, and over all the Northern States; and the American Telegraph Company, having lines in some Southern States and along the sea-coast. About the year 1858 the Western Union had reached this position of telegraphic supremacy, and began its career of glory, power, and dominion.

Its capital was then three hundred and eighty-five thousand seven hundred dollars. During the following eight years it declared upon this insignificant capital stock dividends to the amount of seventeen million eight hundred and ten thousand four hundred and sixty dollars, which, with the issue of some stock for other purposes, raised its capital in 1866 to twenty-two million thirteen thousand seven hundred dollars. In other words, on its capital of three hundred and eighty-five thousand seven hundred dollars it paid during these years an annual average cash and stock dividend of two million seven hundred and forty-five thousand nine hundred and twenty-two dollars.

With this enormous profit of eight years, it was now in a fair condition to swallow its only great rival, the American Telegraph Company, which had a capital of three million eight hundred and thirty-three thousand one hundred dollars. This it paid them, and a bonus of eight million dollars of stock in the Western Union as a dividend.

Then another small company, that had sprung up as a sort of blackmail competition with the Western Union, and which had constructed a few thousand miles of almost worthless lines, had to be put out of the way. The Western Union paid seven million two hundred and sixteen thousand three hundred dollars for these lines, and was and is now the exclusive telegraph company in the United States, having raised its capital from three hundred and eighty-five thousand seven hundred dollars in 1858 to forty-one million sixty thousand one hundred dollars in 1870, on all of which watered stock capital the people who are compelled to make use of the wires have to pay interest, at the high rates asked for the transmission of messages. Thus it happens that while we ought to send off forty million messages per annum in order to be on a par with Belgium, we send off only ten millions. Unable to afford such high rates as our company asks, we use the telegraph only for the most important matters and when it is positively unavoidable. It is simply despotism in this manner to levy so high a tax upon the people for their telegraph business, a despotism which, were it in the nature of a direct tax, a direct extortion, would at once rouse a revolt.

But there is yet another and even worse feature of despotism about this telegraph monopoly that absolutely demands the interference of the government. It is this: being a vehicle of news, the telegraph has and exercises indisputable control over the press and over the publication of news generally. So far as the news generally is concerned, it permits the controllers of the telegraph to speculate on all the political and commercial news that may affect the prices, to withhold, change, or even fabricate dispatches that may involve the fortunes of thousands. No company, no set of men, can be intrusted with such wide-reaching power.

So far as the newspapers of the country are concerned, they are absolutely at the mercy of this monopoly. If they murmur against it, up go the rates, which to the newspaper is the same as off "with its head." Insubordination is thus punished with instant death.

Sooner or later this monopoly must come to an end, and we might as well grapple with it at once. It is the prerogative and duty of the government to take control of all the telegraph lines in the country, or build new ones, and operate them for the exclusive benefit of the people at large. Many improvements can be made in the system, and insulation better attained, so as to secure that speed of transmission which alone makes the telegraph valuable as a means of intercommunication, and yet the rates can be vastly lowered at the same time without loss.

Moreover, as I propose the establishment of a State and national police system, it will become absolutely necessary that the telegraphic communications between all parts of the republic should be controlled exclusively by the government, for the protection of its citizens against fraud and violence, and for the arrest of all guilty parties.

At the same time, since the state itself will become the sole maker of money, leaving gold and silver in their natural condition, to become mere articles of commerce,—in which condition they will soon sink down to their real value,—the post and the telegraph will also become the means of regulating exchanges all over the country. This will have the effect of making exchange par and equal all over the United

States; the slight expense which may occur in balancing the exchanges by the forwarding of actual money going into the general expense account of this department just the same as the printing of the notes, etc.

Ultimately arrangements may also be made with foreign governments to transfer exchanges in this manner by post or telegraph through the international clearing-house.

CHAPTER III.

PUBLIC ROADS.

THE division of our country everywhere into counties, townships, sections, etc., of regular figure, has itself regulated the laying out of highways and roads. Every road should be kept in constant repair and cleanliness, so that the traffic of commerce along the roads in wagons may suffer as little obstruction as possible from the condition of the soil, and that the health of travelers and of residents along the road may not be impaired by clouds of dust or the evaporation of stagnant mud-holes. The double lines of trees along each side of the road will materially contribute to the health and comfort of travelers, and at proper intervals fountains should be put up and places arranged for watering horses and droves of cattle. Every public highway should be put under the constant supervision of road inspectors, who must have power to remedy any defect occurring in the condition of the roads from any cause whatever without the least delay. They must order the making of bridges, durably built, and of a construction to harmonize with the landscape, wherever they shall be necessary, and keep them in constant repair. They must watch and protect the trees along the roads, and be clothed with sufficient police-power to enforce order on the highway. A system of telegraphic communication must be kept up among these inspectors, so that the passage of any drove of cattle, etc., may be known along the road in time to provide against collisions, and for other contingencies.

CHAPTER IV.

RIVERS AND LAKES.

Rivers and lakes constitute natural highways, the right to travel on which must be secured to every citizen. For this purpose it is absolutely necessary that the state should have full control over their navigation, and not leave the traveling public at the mercy of those who make that navigation their special business. No vessel should be allowed, therefore, to enter on this business unless it has been inspected as to its condition and seaworthiness, and such inspection should take place at stated regular periods. Special rules will have to be drawn up for all steam-vessels, so as to secure safety and health to the passengers; the proper ventilation of all berths being an object especially to be looked to. For this purpose every vessel carrying passengers should register the number of passengers to which it is to be limited, and the inspectors will have to see that this rule is not infringed upon. Vessels for the cattle trade must have special arrangements made for the health and cleanliness of the animals.

Wherever any navigable river offers obstructions to navigation it is the duty of the state to remove them, if at all practicable. The old notions of the state holding aloof from internal improvements originated mainly from the great extent of our country, then so thinly populated, which made the vast expenses of such improvements seem too burdensome. Thus what was merely inexpedient for the time being was formulated into a wrong principle; and now that the inexpediency has ceased, the error in the principle has also been laid bare. It is a disgrace to human reason that such vast arteries of commerce as the Mississippi and Missouri should continue to obstruct communication and endanger the safety of navigation, when a judicious system of improvements would place that whole body of water under rational control, and make it an obedient servant, instead of being, as now, an unruly one, full of snags, sawyers, sand-reefs, and other destructive impediments. The same holds good concerning all navigable rivers and lakes, harbors, gulfs, bays, seas, and oceans, whereof surveys should designate all reefs, rocks, and other dangers to navigation.

It is by virtue of making these improvements, and of its obligation to secure to each citizen full protection against the oppressive tyranny of monopolies, that the state exercises the power of regulating commerce and traffic upon rivers and lakes, not only by inspection of and rules concerning the construction of their vessels, etc., but also by establishing such laws as shall prevent the levying of oppressive taxation, in the shape of extravagant rates of freight and passage. For the same tendency to monopoly, and the establishment of powerful and unscrupulous corporations, which has directed the present organization of our railroad system, has manifested, and must necessarily continue to manifest itself, in our system of river and lake navigation. Large, wealthy corporations are organized to build lines of steamers between certain points, and by buying up any threatened competing line that may be proposed, virtually control the whole commerce between those points, levying whatever tax they please upon commerce and the traveling public.

These rivers and lakes being natural highways, the state cannot assume exclusive control of the traffic and travel upon them. But the state is bound to protect its citizens against the oppressive despotism of monopolies, and gains further authority to exercise this protection by undertaking the improvement of these rivers and lakes.

CHAPTER V.

CANALS.

CANALS are artificial water-highways, the possibility of the construction of which depends to a great extent upon the natural river system of the state. Affording far cheaper transportation than railroads, their construction should be encouraged wherever the possibility is offered. They serve, moreover, as natural ventilators, for water-power, for drainage of surface water, and, in some measure, to irrigate the adjoining country. Being the absolute creation of the government,—unlike the rivers,—the government necessarily keeps exclusive control of them, and allows no other private monopoly to build them. How great a benefit a good system of canals is to the people of a state is shown by the Erie Canal, in the State of New York, both directly as a means of transportation, and indirectly as furnishing a marvelous water-power for mills, manufactories, etc.,—a power which cannot, in many instances, be replaced by any other. In still greater measure would their benefit appear in the Southern States, where the winter weather would not interfere with their continuous use.

CHAPTER VI.

RAILROADS.

THAT upon which the life of man hangs as on a thread is time. All that he can secure of it for his own use and enjoyment is in that proportion his own individual and free life. Hence that proportion is his real wealth, and no common sounding saying is more strictly philosophically true than the adage that Time is money. Time is the only money, the only really enjoyable money and wealth, and that which we commonly call money and wealth is only the representative of so much enjoyable time. To secure it to the majority of men in greater proportions than was possible in the past, the invention of man has been at all times busy to gain more time by substituting machinery for labor and for the quicker transportation of persons and property from one part of this world to another. The railway system of communication between one part of the country and all others has thus grown to be of transcendent importance to the welfare of the human race, and the harmonious and fit development of all the faculties of the minds and bodies of the people.

The moneyed powers and monopolies, almost immediately after the discovery of this system of communication, perceived the enormous advantages it would extend to any body of men applying it in a well-populated state, and accordingly prepared to possess themselves of it; the state looking passively on, or if active at all in the matter, applying its activity in the very worst manner, by extending aid gratuitously, in the way of money, credit, lands, etc., to these monopolies, in addition to the enormous privileges conferred upon them by their governmental charters granted by the state.

The reason why the privileges of these railway monopolies are so enormous is this: that of the three elements which enter into the realization of wealth, from its source, the soil,—which are: 1st, production from the soil; 2d, manufacture of the productions for consumption; and 3d, transportation of the manufactured productions to the consumers,—the element of transportation has a double ratio: first, transportation from the producer to the manufacturer; and second, from the manufacturer to the consumer. In addition to this double privilege, which enables transportation to make profits on both trips, the same agency which transports freight can, in the case of railways, be made serviceable to transport passengers.

In this way it has become possible that of the enormous annual revenue of the railroads in our country, which is now estimated at over four hundred million of dollars, about seventy per cent. is used for the expenses of operating those roads, leaving a profit of about thirty per cent., or the enormous sum of one hundred and twenty million dollars per annum on the invested capital. The despotic and corruptive power derived from such vast sums of money income is surely large enough to require all the checks and regulations that legislation can invent, if, indeed, it should not be altogether taken away from private corporations and placed under the immediate control of the state. It was the despotic laying on of taxes by the kings and nobles of France, sucking the life-blood out of the people by their waste, extravagance, and wars, which brought on that terrific revolution we still shudder to read about; and the people of our own country cannot long consent to tolerate this same kind of power in the hands of a few monopolies, exercising it in charging undue rates on freight and passage, and furnishing insufficient accommodation, accompanied with vexatious delays, and often great injuries to persons and property, and the destruction of many lives annually.

The oppression weighs all the more heavily when it is considered that most of these railroads were built with the money of others than the men that now levy those taxes of freight and passage upon the people, nay, to a great extent, with the money of the state itself. Companies have been organized with a large stock account, which never was paid up, while roads were being built by these companies altogether upon a system of mortgages. In other words, a company of men organized under the laws of the state to do a certain thing without subscribing a dollar to do it, and then by trumpeting forth their enterprise to the world fell to mortgaging it in proportion as the money raised by these mortgages paid for the building of the road. If the first mortgage did not suffice to build the road, as it seldom did, second and third mortgages were issued, or construction bonds and equipment bonds. If sufficient mortgages could not be sold to the people in a private way, the State was called upon to make the first loans, which have seldom in that case been repaid, or perhaps even to donate immense tracts of lands, while every town and county along the line of the road was solicited to make additional loans.

Thus the sixteen hundred and thirty-seven miles of the two Pacific railroads were built with a government subsidy of thirty thousand dollars a mile, a mortgage indebtedness of thirty thousand dollars a mile, ever so many State, county, and city loans, and a great land grant of twelve thousand eight hundred acres a mile along the line of the roads; and yet these roads are owned and controlled by the shareholders of the two hundred million dollars of stock that have been issued besides those mortgages, but were never paid up, and were distributed in the main on the Credit Mobilier system.

It is these shareholders, who never built the road, who simply took other people's money, and, making enormous profits out of the construction of the road, helped themselves, moreover, to as much so-called stock as they pleased, that levy annually, through the various railroads of the country, that enormous tax of one hundred and twenty million dollars on the traffic of their roads, besides continuing to enjoy the income of those vast grants of land that have made, to mention only one instance, the Northern Pacific

Railroad the possessor of nearly fifty million acres of land, five hundred and fifty times more than belong to the Duke of Buccleuch, the greatest land-owner in Great Britain.

Furthermore, these shareholders are in most instances not those who projected the original enterprise. The original shares, having been made marketable by their possessors, became immediately a common article of barter, owned to-day by this and to-morrow by that clique of selfish speculators. The temporary owners of the majority of the shares have no permanent interest in the road itself, and their only temporary interest is to make as much as possible out of it.

This leads, of course, to general neglect of the road, resulting in danger to the passengers, and causing those frightful railroad disasters that have been and continue to be the disgrace of our country, suggesting and rendering necessary the establishment of those accident-insurance companies wherein every traveler on a railroad nowadays deems it his duty to invest, before entering a car, for the benefit of his heirs. It furthermore is productive of raising the rates of freight and passage far beyond the requirements of a fair percentage of profit.

It is a matter of course, that every enterprise should, after the payment of all operating expenses, throw off a surplus sufficient to pay a fair interest on the capital invested, besides a legitimate percentage for the risk run in investing it. But the managers of the railroad enterprises discovered, soon after their first introduction, that, being in a position to dictate their own terms to the public, they could make far greater profits than were required by a fair remuneration for capital and risks. They declared dividends so large that they astonished the community, who had to pay these dividends in the way of freight and passage rates.

Naturally, the lawgivers set about to reduce these extortions, and in a manner thereby to regulate freight and passage rates, by passing laws forbidding the monopolies to declare larger dividends than would constitute a very liberal remuneration, say ten per cent. But the monopolies were more cunning than the lawgivers, and the next time their coffers were overrunning from an excess over the ten per cent., took the overrun surplus and divided it among their shareholders as an addition to the capital stock.

Thus was inaugurated that famous system of stock-watering, which has been of late carried to such great perfection in our country; and on every dollar of such watered stock the public must continue to pay additional taxes in the shape of freight and passage rates. It appears by this immediately what extraordinary despotic power these monopolies possess, and how utterly they disregard, by cunning manœuvres, legislative enactments. Though even these they have now grown bold enough to disregard, supremely controlling them, by purchasing the lawmakers beforehand. The Erie Railroad alone boasts of spending one million of dollars per annum in four different States for the purpose of buying the votes of men who will protect its road in the legislature against offensive enactments, and of being able to control at any time twenty-five thousand votes. And yet the Erie controls only seven hundred and seventy miles of railway.

To what extent this "stock-watering" has been carried, and, consequently, to what extent taxes are daily levied upon every passenger and shipper on the railroad, may be gathered from the following figures:

The Erie Railroad in 1862 had a total capital of bonds and debt amounting to $40,285,365. It has since increased it to about $70,000,000.

The New York Central and Hudson River Railroads in 1862 had a total capital of $67,575,039. It has since been increased to $104,661,216.

The Pennsylvania Central Railroad in 1862 had a total capital of $13,724,100. It has since been increased to over $40,000,000.

These are only three roads; but they represent the three greatest enterprises that control the railway commerce of our country. In the case of the Pennsylvania Central, the control extends over more than seven hundred miles of railway; in the case of the Erie Railroad, over seven hundred and seventy-three miles of railway; and in the case of the New York Central, combined as it is now under one management with the Hudson River and Harlem Railways, and, with control of the Lake Shore road, uniting the great commercial metropolis of the Northwest, Chicago, with the commercial metropolis of the country, New York, over some two thousand one hundred and fifty miles of railroad, with an aggregate capital of two hundred and fifteen millions of dollars, and an annual income of forty-five millions of dollars. Let it be remembered that this enormous power is virtually wielded by one man, the same man, moreover, who has already control of the whole telegraph system of the United States, the Western Union, with a capital of some forty-three millions of dollars, and an annual income of probably about three millions of dollars, and with an unlimited control of sixty odd thousand miles of telegraphic communication. This one man, Commodore Vanderbilt, has therefore absolute control over all telegraphic communication between the citizens of the United States and the most important part of their commercial railway communication. He can raise the prices of that intercommunication—that is to say, can levy taxes upon the people who must make use of his railroad and his telegraph—to what extent he chooses; there is no redress at hand. If the legislature attempts to fix the minimum fare on his roads, he can arrange his trains for passengers so that there shall be only one car, or perhaps two cars, on each train, ill constructed, filthy, badly ventilated, and generally uncomfortable, to such a degree that all the passengers feel compelled to enter the drawing-room cars that are attached to the same train, though they have to pay nearly fifty per cent. additional to the legal fare. This same gentleman is now reported to be buying up the Union Pacific Railroad, and thereby extending his power over some sixteen hundred miles more of road. Necessarily the same system will follow, the same stock-watering, and the same increase in the rates. The passengers and shippers of the New York Central Railroad, that in 1862 had to pay rates to meet the requirements of dividends on a capital of only fifty million dollars, have now to pay rates to meet the requirements of dividends on a capital of one hundred and four millions six hundred and sixty-one thousand two hundred and sixteen dollars,—that is to say, the rates which they are made to pay ought to be only one-half of what they are.

No government would dare to oppress the people in the manner that this one monopoly does. The end is inevitable: every railroad in the land must be appropriated by and put under the control of the government. The farmers of the West have already spoken with unmistakable tones in three State elections; it will not be long before the whole nation will take up the same cry.

It was once thought that competition would reduce the extortions of the railroad monopolies to a just rate, and that thus prices would regulate themselves, as from sheer inborn inertness men like to imagine. But far from being so regulated, it soon became apparent that the railroad monopolies were governed by cunning and selfish men, wise enough to take advantage of the indifference and inertness of their fellow-citizens. This they achieved by simply *combining* the competing lines. Of course it was an expensive measure for the established lines, but better than ruin, more especially as the *people* had to pay the expense by increased rates. If any new competing road was planned and undertaken, how quickly the road thereby endangered would buy it up, levying the payment of the purchase-money upon the traveling and commercial public! That it is still worse for the public if the state itself undertakes to establish this competition the railroad history of Massachusetts demonstrates in the most vivid manner in the cases of the Boston, Hartford, and Erie Railroad, and of the Hoosac Tunnel. The state cannot compete with monopolies grown so powerful as the railroads, it must extinguish them by compelling their transfer to the state. Self-preservation demands it, and justice will sanction it. For nearly all of the great roads have been built by the lands and moneys furnished by the state or the people, and public policy requires that the government should control and direct their operations.

Indeed, the extravagant land grants extended to many of these railroad monopolies furnish a sufficient reason for the control of those roads by the government, and the necessity for it is continually increasing. To realize this fully, it should be known that of the one thousand eight hundred and thirty-five million acres of land constituting the United States and Territories, nearly one-fourth is owned by railroad monopolies, an extent of territory larger than France, Spain, Italy, and Great Britain together, while the general reservation for schools to educate ten million scholars was only one-thirty-sixth part of the public lands. All these lands have been given away to build railroads, that by building at double cost—making the average mile cost from sixty to eighty thousand dollars instead of from thirty to fifty thousand dollars per mile, which is the fair legitimate price—levy for all future time upon the traffic of the roads taxes to pay the interest on the additional thirty thousand per mile, and interest besides on the hundreds of million dollars of stock that have been issued as a further fraud.

That is to say, the men who proposed to build the road in a fair way, which would have averaged a cost of about thirty to fifty thousand dollars a mile, organized themselves into another company, Credit Mobilier, or Construction Company, or whatever the chosen name might be, and now built the road at an exorbitant rate of, say sixty to eighty thousand dollars per mile; dividing the immense profit of this construction account among themselves and their friends, besides dividing in a similar manner the fictitious stock which they had caused to be issued.

By those land grants the lands belonging to the people of the United States have been given away in such vast proportions that one of the largest beneficiaries, the Northern Pacific Railroad, in its circular put forth to induce European capitalists to advance money for the construction of the road, has the boldness therein to state: "These lands," the forty-seven million three hundred and sixty thousand acres of the Northern Pacific land grant, "when the road shall be built and the business fairly started, excluding town and station sites, would certainly average ten dollars per acre, making the sum of four hundred and seventy-three million six hundred thousand dollars. Supposing the construction of the road should cost sixty thousand dollars per mile, the entire cost at this rate would be one hundred and twenty million dollars, leaving to the shareholders an excess of clear profit from the lands alone of three hundred and fifty-three million six hundred thousand dollars."

That is to say, the Congress of the United States has given to this one corporation three hundred and fifty-three million six hundred thousand dollars of estimated profit for building a road which that corporation did not advance a single dollar to build, borrowing all the money required in advance on the lands thus stolen from the people. That corporation took no risk, a guaranteed profit by its own confession of three hundred and fifty-three million six hundred thousand dollars, the vast profits made in building the road at an estimated cost of sixty thousand dollars per mile, when it ought to be about thirty thousand dollars, and now holds its immense power in perpetual danger to and oppression of the people. That the people are the equitable owners of the road, having paid for it in full, and three hundred and fifty-three million six hundred thousand dollars profit to the corporation besides, is clear, and yet they will have no share in the ownership, and will be charged exorbitant rates of freight and passage,—that is to say, will be taxed to whatever enormous amount the payment of interest on the mortgages, of dividends on unpaid stock, and of other fraudulent Credit Mobilier charges, shall render it advisable and profitable to the company to make.

Thus Congress has given away about one-fourth of its public lands to two gigantic corporations, composed of perhaps one hundred stockholders, conferring upon them rights and privileges the richest dukes and princes of Europe might be proud of; and yet it has assigned but one-thirty-sixth part of those lands to the ten million children who now demand education, and whose number will soon reach twenty or forty millions of souls. Can any one doubt, in view of these facts, that the most vital interests of the people have been betrayed by Congress for the aggrandizement of the railroad kings, whose patents of sovereignty are contained in those acts of our congressional parliament granting the vast domains of the people to monopolizing despotisms, whose powers for illegal taxation will produce extortions that have been rivaled only in the Roman provinces in the most corrupt days of the Roman republic?

Another danger resulting from this insane alienation of the people's rich domains is this. The population of the United States is now about forty millions, some twelve millions of which are agriculturists. There are left to the United States of its one billion eight hundred and thirty-four million nine hundred and ninety-eight thousand four hundred acres, some three hundred and seventy million of which are in Alaska, only in the neighborhood of eight hundred million acres of land for our future agricultural population. When will this be exhausted? Estimating every one hundred and sixty acres capable of supporting five persons, the eight hundred million acres will be absorbed when our agricultural population shall have been increased from twelve to sixty millions,—that is to say, when our whole population shall have risen to about one hundred and twenty millions, which is certainly no very remote future, being likely to occur, according to calculations based on the progress of the past, before half a century. This matter gains all the more importance from the fact that the productiveness of our lands is decreasing to such an extent as to make—what seems now an impossibility—seasons of famine in the United States quite likely to occur by that time, unless, indeed, our agriculturists engage the aid of science in their behalf, and by the establishment of such agricultural schools as I have proposed, learn to make the soil yield artificially the same as it yielded when it was first opened by man.

It is only by experience that the danger from monopolies shows itself. In the infancy of the railroad system in the United States no trouble was apprehended from it, but now that the system has grown to extend from two thousand miles in 1840 to about sixty-seven thousand one hundred and four miles in 1873,—as great a length for our forty million of people as Europe has for her three hundred million,—and when thirty-five thousand miles more are now in course of construction, the danger has grown so imminent that it were suicide on the part of our republic to tolerate its uncontrolled domination any longer.

In Belgium the government has already secured itself against this danger by obtaining control of all the railroads in the country; in France this policy has also been followed, though in a partial way; in England the proposition to have the government obtain control of all the railroads is growing daily into more favor. In our own country, which is threatened so much more by these monopolies than the kingdoms and empires of Europe, owing to the immensely more extensive development of the railway system, the farmers and shippers of the West are just beginning to rise in opposition to an intolerable tyranny; and yet so extensive is the power of these railroad monopolies, that scarcely any of the leading newspapers of the country—generally so apt to espouse a popular cause—have dared to lend their support to this most important and significant movement.

For all these reasons, as well because it is the duty of the government to control all public highways and afford to each citizen the speediest access to all others, as because the government can build roads cheaper than any private company, having larger credit and greater means, and can operate them more economically, as is shown by the United States management of the post-office, I propose that the government should take control of the whole railway system and manage it for the benefit of the whole people, as has been done in Belgium with such marked success. The time has gone by for keeping the limits of government within the sphere of merely protecting the liberties of the people against direct violence, for indirect fraud and extortions have assumed proportions that threaten to swallow up all liberties. When corporations can grow so powerful that they may with impunity, as the Erie road did, and as the New York Central did, though in a less open way, plunder and oppress the unprotected public, bribe the law-makers of the state, make war upon each other, absorb permanently, by greater salaries than the state will afford to pay, the most eminent legal talent, and by their indirect influence, as well as by direct corruption, gain over the power of the courts, no government that values its existence can look on with indifference. Neither the Erie clique alone nor the Tammany clique alone could have perpetrated their huge frauds successfully; it was the combination of both, supported, moreover, by all the other great monopolies and corporations that depended equally upon a rule of fraud and violence, which made possible the disgraceful scenes of recent times.

To tamper with these railroad companies by reorganizing them as legally existing monopolies and regulating their charges, mode of doing business, etc., in short, to make a special contract with each, may allay some of the worst features of our present system, but it is no radical cure, and, moreover, nourishes other evils,—such as bribery of the legislative bodies. Special legislation is always a danger, and besides is calculated to deceive the public, by a *quasi* legislative indorsement of the enterprises it charters.

What we need is, that the state should assume control of all the railroads, fix their capital stock permanently, thereby rooting out the worst of stock speculation, and run them at the lowest possible rate compatible with a fair interest and dividend, in the interest of the people alone, and pay the present owners a just compensation. All that has been said of the steam railways in this chapter applies equally to the horse railways, etc., that afford communication to the inhabitants of large cities. They should all be under the direct control of the respective municipal corporations.

This change in the administration of the railways should be accompanied by a radical change in their management. Every steam railway should have a double track, and the most complete system of signals, etc., that human ingenuity can devise to prevent collisions. No car should be heated in any other way than by hot-water pipes, nor lighted with combustible oils; and a complete system of ventilation should be arranged for every passenger car and for all cars used for the transportation of animals. Every car should be arranged for a fixed number of passengers, and no overcrowding should be allowed. The cars for the transportation of animals should also be limited to a definite number of the various classes of animals, and be so constructed as to allow them sufficiency of air, water, and food. At the same time the road-beds should be so made, and the machinery of the locomotives as well as the construction of the cars so devised, under the guidance of science, as to insure the speediest as well as safest transmission of persons and property.

TAXATION, DUTIES AND IMPOSTS.

CHAPTER I.

THE NATURE OF TAXATION.

WHEN the people of a certain district, territory, or state gather themselves into a political unity for the purpose of securing to each citizen his right to life, freedom, and property, and thereby his right to the fit and harmonious use of all the faculties of his mind and body, they establish a government to carry out their purpose. This government requires—1st, money salaries for the persons composing it, since they have no other means of support; and 2d, money for the execution of those measures the government considers essential to carry out its purposes and execute the law. In private associations such money, salaries, and expenses are obtained from the profits of the associations, and deducted before the declaration of a dividend.

Government, however, does not propose to make any profit, redivisible among its citizens, but simply to conduct all its functions on the most economical basis. It does not propose to make out of its postal, railroad, and other functions money enough to pay its own expenses, since such a course would be manifestly unjust to the majority of the people. It is, therefore, bound to assess all the expenses of its administration upon the whole people indiscriminately, which assessment is called taxation.

The problem arises here: How is that taxation to be levied justly and impartially upon all values alike in the same proportion?

It is one of the old legal superstitions that only land is real property, and hence that its possession must be the basis of all taxation. This superstition had its origin in the feudal arrangement of assessing each vassal a specified number of warriors according to the extent and population of his landed property, the landed proprietors alone being considered worthy of direct taxation.

Moses did not make use of this inequitable species of taxation; he simply levied a capitation tax of a half shekel on every male in the nation, besides a tribute of the first fruits and the first born of all domestic animals, together with tithes for the support of the priestly tribe of the Levites, and every third year a tithe for the support of the poor. It is, moreover, to be observed that the undue increase of these taxes under the kings, when the organic law of Moses had already lost much of its supremacy, and when thus taxes began to be levied upon lands, houses, and foreign merchandise, assisted in the final utter overthrow of the Mosaic code, and the secession of the ten tribes, which, a few centuries after, was followed by the scattering of the Jewish people over the world.

Neither in the Greek nor in the Roman republics were taxes ever levied. They supported their organizations, as we have already seen, by the plunder of war; and it was only in the later times of the Roman empire that divers kinds of levies were practiced to meet the enormous expenses of its rulers.

But in the feudal times a king levied upon his subordinate princes, whenever war was necessary, according to the terms of their feudal lien, and had to recover his other necessaries from his own domains and the plunder obtained by the war. The noble landed possessors again covered their expenses by divers arrangements with their freeholders, tenants, slaves, etc., or, if very noble, by plundering whoever fell into their hands, and particularly the Jews.

But it is very evident that thus to consider land as the only real taxable property is a wrong and unjust procedure. Take a farmer who owns a farm, say worth eight thousand dollars, its annual income being five hundred dollars. You assess him as worth, say six thousand dollars, it being a foolish rule always to assess at about one-third less than the actual value. Next you call upon a physician who has an extensive practice. He has no real property, none at all. Hence you do not assess him. Nevertheless the physician has an annual income of say ten thousand dollars.

This is flagrant injustice. The farmer has land worth five hundred dollars a year, and the physician has an income from his practice worth ten thousand dollars a year; and yet under that system the latter pays no tax, while the former pays an exorbitant one, simply because his property is in land. The unjust inequality becomes still more glaring where, in some States, if the farmer has mortgaged his land, worth eight thousand dollars, for six thousand dollars, he pays, nevertheless, taxes upon the whole value, where his interest in it is only two thousand dollars. The farmer's land is nothing more than a source of revenue, like the practice of the physician; in either case the income should be taxed. If a person has other real estate than that from which he derives income, and holds it unimproved and without leasing it if practicable, he may be taxed for the income it would bring if used or leased.

Taxation to be just should be primarily assessed, according to the respective net incomes of all citizens, to be ascertained as stated. Thus the farmer should pay taxes upon his income, and not upon the real estate from which it is produced; the manufacturer no taxes upon his factory, machinery, stock material, capital used, or his dwelling-house; nor the physician upon his office, library, medicines, or dwelling-house; and the reasonable necessary expenses of carrying on such business, or the practice of a physician, should be deducted from the gross income in all cases, the true rule being to tax net income only.

But where such assessment is made upon the unproductive wealth of citizens, that assessment should be made upon the real value, since every other form must prove unjust, and cannot bear equally upon all.

As things are at present, we assess the thirty thousand millions of our whole national wealth at only fourteen billion one hundred and seventy-eight million nine hundred and eighty-six thousand seven hundred and thirty-two dollars. That this must operate great wrong on many is evident. Massachusetts, for instance, paying taxes on one billion five hundred and ninety-one million dollars of its computed wealth of two billion one hundred and thirty-two million dollars, is greatly wronged if New York pays taxes on one billion nine hundred million dollars, when the real value of her wealth is six billion five hundred million dollars, and similar injustice cannot fail to occur in the assessments of individual citizens in the separate States.

The assessment made upon the income, however, should include all income, and no source of income should ever be exempted by law from taxation. It is directly violative of all justice to exempt from taxation certain bonds, bearing interest, or any other property, thereby establishing among the taxpayers a privileged class or a moneyed aristocracy. It was bad enough to sell our interest-bearing bonds, in many instances, at only one-half their par value,—bonds that bore heavy interest, and that have since been unjustly made payable—both capital and interest—in gold; but it was an additional outrage upon the people to exempt these bonds from taxation. This has created a privileged class in our republic, utterly inconsonant with the principles of a just government, bearing equally upon all citizens.

CHAPTER II.

THE TRUE RULES OF TAXATION.

ADAM SMITH lays down the maxims of taxation in this manner:

1. "The subjects of every state ought to contribute toward the support of the government, as nearly as possible, in proportion to their respective abilities,—that is, *in proportion to the revenue which they respectively enjoy under the protection of the state*."

2. "The tax which each individual is bound to pay ought to be certain, and not arbitrary; the time of payment, the manner of payment, and the quantity to be paid, ought all to be clear and plain to the contributor and to every other person."

3. "Every tax ought to be levied at the time and in the manner in which it is most likely to be convenient for the contributor to pay it."

4. "Every tax ought to be so contrived as both to take out and keep out of the pockets of the people as little as possible over and above what it brings into the public treasury of the state."

These maxims are so manifestly just that they ought not to stand in need of any arguments in their support. The only equal taxation is that which is levied in proportion to the revenue which citizens respectively enjoy under the protection of the state,—that is to say, upon their income. And not only is it the only equal and just mode, but it also excludes arbitrariness in the assessment, and makes it always distinctly known to every person how much his taxes will amount to.

It is, furthermore, the only mode of taxation which can be so regulated that it can be levied at the time most convenient to the tax-payer, and which admits of the cheapest system of collection. Under our present systems of collecting taxes and duties, the cost of collecting, in many instances, equals the amount collected.

CHAPTER III.

THE LIMITS OF TAXATION.

Taxation should be levied only for the needs of the government to carry out its functions, and for no other purpose whatever.

Under the present state of things the larger amount of the taxes goes in a direct or indirect way towards the payment of interest on the bonds, mortgages, and loans negotiated by the general government, or the several States, counties, and cities. By the adoption of the money-system I propose, and which is the only system founded upon a rational basis and comprehension of the real nature of money, this larger amount of taxes would in a very short time cease to oppress the people.

For with the establishment of such a money-system by the general government the prohibition of the issue of further bonds by the several States, counties, cities, etc., would necessarily go hand in hand, since such issue would interfere with the money-making power of the general government, as has already been shown. Nor, indeed, as the whole past history of our cities, counties, and States has shown, is there any occasion for the issue of such bonds. With rare exceptions those loans have been contracted in the behalf of upstarting monopolies, railroads, or other enterprises, that, as soon as thus nourished into wealth, have turned around and become a curse to the cities, counties, and States that cherished them. The railroad history of Missouri, Tennessee, and North Carolina is full of wholesome lessons in this respect. The financial history of New York City is a still more frightful lesson in the same direction, as to the folly and danger of permitting cities this prerogative of money making by the issue of bonds. Had New York City had no power to borrow money on her bonds the Tweed infamy would have been impossible, and the citizens of to-day and of an indefinite future would not be saddled with a debt of a hundred millions, the taxes on which constitute about the largest item in the whole tax list. Indeed, it may be safely said that the taxes paid by the people during the last ten years in the way of interest alone on the loans contracted by their respective States, counties, and cities, would have sufficed to make all the improvements for which the loans were originally contracted. It is this interest which is the heaviest tax, the real money-despot, which is to be abolished. In the general government its power will be abolished by issuing paper money to redeem interest-bearing bonds; in the States, counties, and cities, it will be suppressed by prohibiting their power to contract loans, except from the federal government for the purposes of liquidation.

The individual alone, who chooses to put himself under its rule, may of course do so, but for the consequences he has only himself to blame. Few individuals are, however, likely to be so imprudent in their private affairs. It is only through the indirect agency of the state that men are guilty of these things. Men who would rebel at the least direct taxation are quite ready indirectly to tax themselves to any extent, whether through the agency of interest, or of the tariff.

CHAPTER IV.

THE TARIFF.

For the tariff is nothing but precisely such another indirect mode of taxation, and has its chief support in the absurd reluctance of men to look things boldly in the face and tax themselves directly for their necessary expenses. The other notion which sustains it, that it is a means of protection to the manufactures of a state, is simply an error of judgment; but the notion that it is a legitimate means of raising revenue is sheer absurdity. Both of these notions will have to be swept away with all other superstitions; and commerce between nations must be made as free as it is between our separate States, and as it was originally, before despots found it a very effective means in an indirect way to increase the revenues of direct taxation and plunder.

So far as our own country is concerned, we can effect this even now, at any time. It only needs courage. So far as other nations are concerned, the adoption of my international code by such nations as are desirous to join the proposed international federation would surely pave the way for free trade over the whole extent of the globe. The Geneva arbitration, in its settlement of the fishery question, has already shown—what, indeed, Cobden's Anglo-French alliance had before demonstrated—that this is not a visionary proposition, but easily made actual, and sure to result in prosperity for the people.

Indeed, it may be laid down as an axiom, that the prosperity of a country increases in proportion as all shackles on commerce and interchange between men are removed. The issue of paper money, such as I propose, is one of the means to remove them; the control of railroads, establishment of canals, and improvements of rivers and lakes is another; and the abolition of all duties in every shape is the third. It has so proved in the cases of England and France, as it has proved in our own case among the several States.

Originally the tariff-system was adopted by the founders of our republic in order to pay, by its means, all the expenses of government without making the then new Union odious in the minds of the people by a direct taxation. It was this fear of directness which led to its establishment and continuance. During the war of 1812 duties were increased to pay the expenses resulting from it; but soon after they were again lowered; and this policy was continued until 1860, when the average duties did not exceed fourteen per cent., a little higher than those of Great Britain; whereas now the average duties are fifty per cent., or nearly four times as much,—a most excessive and burdensome tax, levied in a burdensome manner upon the people, and costing many millions to collect.

It was the late civil war that again led to this excessive increase of duties, which now average fifty per cent. on all dutiable articles, and weigh most oppressively upon the laboring classes of the country. Nor were the manufacturing interests slow to avail themselves of this new policy, and to accumulate vast fortunes by the profits thus opened to them.

These profits were naturally a tribute levied upon the people that had to purchase the manufactured wares. The people thus had to pay, and continue to pay, a double tax: one to the government in the shape of duties, and another one to the manufacturers in the shape of increased cost of productions.

It is this inequitable phase of the tariff that has made it so odious as finally to arouse the people to emphatic protest against its continuance, and to a demand for the immediate removal of all shackles upon the commercial intercommunication of the various nations of the world.

To illustrate: In the State of Illinois there are three hundred and seventy-six thousand four hundred and forty-one persons engaged in agriculture, and fifty-eight thousand eight hundred and fifty-two in manufacture, while in the State of Massachusetts two hundred and seventy-nine thousand three hundred and eighty persons are engaged in manufacture, and only seventy-two thousand eight hundred and ten cultivate farms. The total value of all the products of the three hundred and seventy-six thousand four hundred and forty-one Illinois farmers for the year 1870 is estimated at two hundred and ten million eight hundred and sixty thousand five hundred and eighty dollars, thus averaging the annual earnings of every farmer at five hundred and sixty dollars. For the same year the total value of all the products of two hundred and seventy-nine thousand three hundred and eighty manufacturers of Massachusetts is estimated at five hundred and fifty-three million nine hundred and twelve thousand five hundred and sixty-eight dollars, which leaves a remainder, after deducting the estimated value of materials used in the manufactures, three hundred and thirty-four million four hundred and thirteen thousand nine hundred and eighty-two dollars, of two hundred and nineteen million four hundred and ninety-eight thousand five hundred and eighty-six dollars, or an average annual earning of each manufacturer of seven hundred and forty-nine dollars.

Now this would be perfectly fair and legitimate if the manufacturer of Massachusetts sold his wares at the same price at which the Illinois farmer could procure them from other sources. But this he does not. He sells them for about fifty per cent. higher rates, and the United States government enables him to do so successfully by imposing a tariff of such percentage upon foreign wares of similar kind that seek a market here. The United States government thereby compels the Illinois farmer, whose annual earnings are only five hundred and sixty dollars, to pay the Massachusetts manufacturer an average of fifty per cent. more than a fair price upon his wares, in order that his annual earnings may realize seven hundred and forty-nine dollars. This is certainly not an equal administration of the law, and, besides being unjust, tends to the creation of those large manufacturing monopolies that, in the Eastern States, threaten the liberties of the people as much as the railway monopolies threaten those of the agricultural and commercial communities, and that grow powerful, as has been shown, by the indirect tax which a tariff enables them to levy upon the people at large by the increased price of their products.

But even in this protective element of the tariff its intended effect in some cases overleaps itself, and becomes ruinous both to the manufacturer and the consumer. Perhaps the most striking instance is that of wools and woolen goods, the duties on which now average at the enormous figures of from fifty to one hundred and fifty per cent. ad valorem. If this duty did really protect manufacturers, how could it have come to pass that woolen industry was never so depressed as at present, and that more people than ever wear woolen goods imported from foreign countries?

If the tariff really effected what it was intended to effect, the fostering of our manufacturing interests, how could it happen that in no recent period in the history of the United States have we had less exports and more imports than now? The products of manufactures that we export now are scarcely worth mentioning. Of the one hundred and seventy-six million dollars increase of exports from 1860 to 1872, one hundred and seventy million dollars were composed of breadstuffs, coin, provision, lumber, etc., leaving only six million dollars of manufactured wares for those years under the operation of the high protective tariff that was to effect such magnificent results. Even our export of shoes has fallen off, despite the wonderful progress that has been made of late years in their manufacture. Thus instead of making us more independent in industrial matters of Europe, the effect worked by a high tariff has been precisely the reverse, besides ruining our whole commercial marine, lowering the percentage of carriage of foreign trade by our ships from seventy-one per cent. in 1860 to only about thirty per cent. in 1871.

Our trade with Southern Africa and La Plata is broken up because we cannot import the wool of those countries at the enormous duty now levied on it, and our ships cannot afford to carry there petroleum, fish, flour, etc., unless they have a return cargo. Our ships cannot go to Spain, Italy, West India, etc., because we cannot import salt with the present tariff, although imported salt is far superior to our own for the preservation of meat and fish. The importation of wool fell from eighty-eight million pounds in 1864 to twenty-three millions in 1868, and the importation of salt from four hundred and six thousand to two hundred thousand tons in the same time.

There ought to be really no dispute on this point. Historically, it was the principle of free trade which proved the most efficient agent in bringing the people of the old Confederacy to adopt the plan of the new Union. No argument appealed with so tangible a force to their apprehension of the vast benefits that must result from the Union as this one of the removal of all restrictions upon commerce between the several States of the Union in the way of duties and imposts. This great principle of free trade has since then extended from thirteen to our present forty-seven States,—States as industrially different from each other as they are when compared with foreign states, and embracing all classes and conditions of labor, and still the same grand results of prosperity and comfort have followed it. No principle, again, was so effective in arousing the people at the outbreak of the civil war to resist the secession of any part of the country than this of free trade, and the consequent fear of having clogs put on the wheels of commercial intercourse by the success of the secession movement. The whole West protested against the notion of breaking up free trade on the Mississippi River. It would be a paradox to repudiate that principle in its application to foreign states.

Again, when the city of Chicago was burnt in that great conflagration, from the ruins of which it has in so short a time sprung up again in greater strength and beauty than before, the people of the suffering city immediately petitioned Congress to remove the protective duties on all the articles needed in the rebuilding, thereby acknowledging at once the great relief which that removal would extend to them. What grand benefits would be realized by all mankind if that removal of duties upon commerce could be made universal over the whole world, and thereby a main source of international hostility be removed! The adoption of my proposition for an international federation would doubtless bring this result about in a very short time, for every nation would perceive the immense advantages of universal free trade upon its prosperity and wealth.

Meanwhile in our own country it is within our power to take the initial step by abolishing our whole tariff system, with its frauds and oppressions and creations of monopolies, as soon as we are able to pay off or redeem our bonds with the money of the country, to be issued for that purpose, as I have proposed should be done at the earliest day possible.

INTERCOMMUNICATION BY THE PRESS.

CHAPTER I.

THE PRESS.

THE original conception of a newspaper was, as its name indicates, that of a publication which should contain the authentic and latest news of public interest that could be ascertained and collected for circulation. Prior to the invention of types for printing, such papers were written and copied for distribution, necessarily to a very limited extent. But since the discovery of the art of printing and the application of steam as a motive-power for the printing-press, the publication and circulation of newspapers has assumed vast proportions, as a general means for intercommunication between all citizens and peoples.

This most wonderful discovery of modern times for the general dissemination of intelligence throughout the world has multiplied the old methods of communicating ideas and news more than a million-fold, illumining the darkest districts of the world, and opening to the people a new era of universal intelligence, instruction, and progress. So long as it was managed for the dissemination of truthful information its influence was always in favor of the freedom of the human race; but in so far as the press was a mighty power for good, it was equally one for evil.

The extraordinary extension of the circulation of printed newspapers was accompanied by a great change in their nature and character. Formerly, men who, from their high culture and wisdom, felt authorized to give publicity to their individual opinions, did so in pamphlets, over their own signatures. The newspapers had not then become the subsidized advocates of monopolies and partisans, and attempted no control over public opinion for private personal aggrandizement or persecution, and the pamphlets essayed no further influence than the legitimate use of their facts or arguments justified. Their readers were invited only to the exercise of self-thinking and individual judgment.

CHAPTER II.

THE DEMORALIZATION OF THE PRESS.

DURING that first period of its existence, while the newspaper remained the faithful advocate of the eternal truths of human liberty and progress, and the medium of truthful news from all parts of the world, it was a great public blessing. It then had no essential connection with the publisher, who was only expected to have a talent for the organization of news gathering, and the editorial columns were open to the most learned men and scholars of the age for comments upon all new discoveries, reforms, and other matters of public concern; but as the circulation of the newspapers extended,—partly owing to an increased desire of the people for the latest news and partly to the introduction of business advertisements,—and as their proprietors thus grew rich and powerful, it occurred to them to increase their power, by making the newspaper not only a vehicle for news, but also for partisan comment upon all questions. This was especially notable in those countries that encouraged opposing political parties, like France, England, and the United States.

Thus the owner of an established journal would increase the circulation of his paper by permitting it to become the "organ" of a political party; or some ambitious partisan would purchase or set up a newspaper to communicate his views and direct the judgment and opinions of the multitude for his own aggrandizement; both parties accomplishing their objects under the impersonal name and character of a "Globe," "Post," "World," "Times," "Enquirer," "Argus," etc.

When this state of things began to develop itself, the issuing of pamphlets, wherein important political questions could be discussed in a thorough and statesmanlike manner, gradually ceased, and in their place came the flippant, abusive, scurrilous, and irresponsible editorial. It is only in France that this department retained character and responsibility, in the requirement of having the author's name attached to every article.

In Great Britain and the United States, however, the editorial was used to a great extent simply as a party instrument, and, as its license grew by toleration, became soon a means whereby to vent all the personal favoritism or malice which the proprietor or his friends might entertain towards any one or any party.

The inherent love of scandal, of reading vile charges against a neighbor, which animates all base characters, lent a support to this department of the newspaper, and in course of time made it a prominent feature. The paper now was read not only for the news it contained, but for the malice of its editorials or the spitefulness of its local paragraphs. Private life became grossly and indecently exposed to public animadversion in the press, and the most insignificant scribbler of items usurped the power to make a sensitive person's existence insupportable, and to destroy the best man's reputation by continued scurrilous mention. This sort of newspaper poisoning and assassination has grown so common, and is carried on so audaciously by mendacious, blackmailing, piratical newspaper buccaneers, that our noblest minds and best scholars shrink from entrance into public life as from a pest-house.

Whenever a growing despotism or monopoly intends to usurp powers that are granted to no individual person, it hides its serpent's coils under the mask of an assumed impersonal name. The editors of this class of newspapers found this impersonal feature ready at hand in the title of their organs. This feature they therefore retained and impressed into their use. It was no longer the individual Mr. A or B who uttered an opinion upon matters modestly over his own name, but an impersonal oracle, a "Mercury," or "Sun," or "Independent," that thundered forth its denunciations with the tone of an inspired prophet, and as the legitimate and recognized expounder of universal public opinion.

The unknown always excites fear; all superstition has its root in and thrives upon this cowardly fear of the unknown. Now the newspaper has become, in its worst specimens, very similar in its terrors to such an unknown power,—of uttering, in grandiloquent phrases, its hurtful praise, its ill-considered judgments, its slanders of good men, and its personal malice.

One needs but to turn over some of the specimens of this class of papers of the past, and glance at the venomous slanders and scandals raised against Washington, Jefferson, Madison, Hamilton, Paine, Adams, Jackson, Webster, Calhoun, Clay, Benton, and others of our noblest patriots, to realize the extent of shamelessness to which this was carried on. Nor was there any redress; for if any outraged person appealed to the law for protection, the newspapers of this class, however much opposed to each other before, straightway combined to raise a hue and cry against the injured man, as one who would interfere with the "liberty of the press!"

For this impersonal title of "the press" had been invented and was now used to cover the multitudinous impersonalities of all newspapers whatsoever, uniting them for popular effect under one general organization, claiming immunity from all control of the law; and thus a few publishers and editors of that class—few in comparison with the millions of other citizens—were gradually allowed to usurp a license and tyranny which has become one of the most distressing features of our age. Not only does it deter the wisest and purest men of our nation from entering into public life, but it enables demagogues to take State and federal offices, upon pledges that they will support the monopolists, the party, and "the press."

In monarchical countries the governments no sooner became aware of the despotism of "the press" than they hastened to check it by an exercise of their own tyrannic power, either by suppressing the newspapers or establishing a censorship over them. As a further protection, they have frequently established official newspapers of their own.

But in our country the worst class of such newspapers have had the broadest scope for mischief imaginable, each party organ endeavoring, to the best of its ability, to misrepresent the actual news or facts when considered adverse to its own interests or the interests of its supporters, and imposing upon its readers by the assumption of the royal "WE," as if it were the sole organ of "the press." At the same time the indiscriminate publication of all sorts of so-called news, consisting chiefly of reports of immoral fictions, of adultery, seductions, rapes, robberies, and murders, has had such a tendency to deprave the minds of the people, brutalize their tastes, familiarize them with crime, and confuse their moral judgments, as to excite the liveliest apprehensions of all good men, parents, and guardians concerning its demoralizing effects upon the rising generation.

True, there have been at all times, and now are, many noble exceptions in "the press," just as there are among the money and railway despots; but I have described the general system of partisan publication, it being the object of this work to expose all forms of despotism and monopoly, and their principal agencies, under whatever cloak they may try to hide themselves.

To what extent the evils attendant upon this form

of abuse of public intercommunication by "the press" can be checked and punished by law will be considered in a subsequent work, as coming within the sphere of the negative application of our fundamental principle, under the head of libel, in State and federal codes of laws. These historical and critical remarks have been made simply with a view to introduce to public consideration an important affirmative duty of a rational state organization; the duty of perfecting the public intercommunication between its citizens by the publication of daily official newspapers, so as to furnish them an authentic history of the events of each day, without editorial comments, and without any charge or expense to the citizens.

CHAPTER III.

A DAILY NATIONAL NEWSPAPER.

It is the duty of government to make known all its laws, official and judicial decisions, and public proceedings, at the earliest possible moment, to all its citizens, since no one should be required to obey laws of which he has had no reasonable opportunity to inform himself. And when the government assumes, as I propose it should, control of all the methods of transmitting news, it becomes a duty for it to make known to the citizens at once all the news communicated from any part of the world.

Government ought not to leave this important branch of intercommunication to private citizens or monopolies, whose self-interest or corrupt motives may be in direct opposition to the welfare of the people; partly for its own sake, since it is primarily interested in a continuous and reliable transmission of news from all parts of the world, and partly because it is bound to protect the people against false information or imposition on matters so important to their general welfare.

The government of the United States should therefore establish a daily newspaper publication, by means of which to make known to all citizens—firstly, all measures, decisions, laws, proceedings, and accounts of its various departments, so that no one can plead ignorance of their existence or be debarred from the strictest scrutiny into their nature; and secondly, all the news that may be transmitted by mail or telegraph to the various departments of the government.

By such a daily publication, all the official acts of our government and of foreign governments concerning the public interests, stock quotations, prices of products, etc.; each new financial regulation, every change in the money issue, all new laws made or proposed to be made, all acts, decisions, measures, and proceedings of the various departments, offices, and bureaus, all governmental contracts, all accounts of expenses classified for publication at stated intervals, all sales of public lands, of property, etc.; all patent rights granted, extended, or renewed, all advertisements of contracts, the weekly imports and exports, and other matters appertaining to the administration of our public affairs, would be accurately communicated to the public at large in the most authentic and prompt manner. Moreover, all the scientific discoveries of the universities, academies of science, State and national institutions, etc., all reports of weather, of electric and magnetic phenomena, of scientific, educational, hygienic, and commercial news, analytically classified and indexed at stated periods, would thus be made immediately and generally known.

Such a national newspaper, therefore, in addition to furnishing the people with accurate statements of all news and events transpiring in the world, would give publicity to all the expenses, income, contracts, and transactions of all departments of the government, and enable the citizens to detect all errors, extravagance, and defalcations in official statements of accounts, whereby the present alarming frauds perpetrated on all sides would be effectually arrested and prevented.

By this simple measure of giving the public full knowledge of all official operations, and three months notice of all new laws proposed to be presented at the next succeeding session of Congress, the whole rotten system of class legislation, moreover, would be terminated, and the principal causes of official demoralization removed.

In like manner, each State and populous municipal corporation should have a daily newspaper, to be conducted upon similar principles and for the same objects, without any editorial comments. It is the truth the people want, and they should be protected from the organized mendacity of the corrupt portion of "the press" by a truthful publication of all matters of public concern, so that they may form their own opinions, and examine thoroughly for themselves all questions, accounts, and things whatsoever concerning the operations of the State and federal governments.

POLICE, PASSPORTS, REGISTRATION.

I.

The object of the criminal laws of the state is to secure the citizens against fraud and violence, by providing for the arrest and punishment of offenders. The object of a police system is to prevent the fraud or violence from being committed, and also to aid in the arrest of all criminals. It is far more important to the welfare of citizens that an offender should be prevented from committing a crime than suffer punishment after its commission. Hence the purely negative code must be aided by a positive one, establishing such regulations as may be necessary to render the commission of offenses almost impossible. Such a positive code is called police law, the law of prevention.

Every well-regulated state is, therefore, bound to establish such a police law and organize a special department, of police, passports, and registration, to carry out its provisions. In proportion as this department is conducted so as to be most effective and least oppressive, will it best subserve the purposes of its creation. Its very objects require it to be exacting, and to demand from all citizens an observance and obedience to all regulations that are essential to carry out its purpose to prevent crime. For men cannot penetrate the motives of others, or foresee the designs of strangers coming into a neighborhood, unless they know the antecedents of such strangers, their residence, occupation, age, name, and purposes. For this reason the police must be empowered to ascertain these facts and verify them, and all persons should be required to submit to the necessary precautionary examination, whether they have any criminal intent or not. Such a thorough police department is particularly necessary in our States. Free of access and open to all new-comers, as all our counties and cities are,—no inquiry being anywhere raised as to the real name, character, or occupation of the new resident,—crime enjoys here unusual advantages and immunities, and not only are many crimes committed, but in most cases the criminals escape or go unpunished. On the other hand the individual efforts that have been made to prevent and punish crime by the organization of private police corporations, styled "Detective Agencies," have but too generally succeeded in defeating the purposes for which they were created. For being under no control of the government, and owing no reports to the law, their whole aim and object has been to make as much money as possible,—an aim and object utterly incompatible with the conception of a true police system. This has worked great wrong in two ways:—Firstly, it has led to the vicious habit of compounding felony with nearly every criminal whose position in life, adroitness, and extent of theft made this the most profitable arrangement; the defaulter or robber of three hundred thousand dollars, for instance, retaining one hundred thousand dollars, and restoring two hundred thousand dollars to the party robbed, who is rejoiced to get back two-thirds of his stolen property, even though he have to pay, say fifty thousand dollars of it, to the detective agency that so cleverly managed the business. Secondly, it has led to the extension of the odious system of blackmailing, beyond any limit before thought possible. The detective agency, being purely a money-making establishment, naturally set all its sharp wits to work to discover new ways of making money and adding to the dividends of the detective corporation. It quickly discovered a very remunerative way of this sort, in setting its agents to pry into the private affairs of people; and from the scandal thus collected, to select such information concerning shy and easily frightened people as might produce large rewards if the publication of the scandal were withheld.

It is quite true that the organization of a state police which shall at once fulfill its functions effectively, and yet leave to the individual unimpaired freedom under the law, is one of the most delicate tasks intrusted to the lawgiver, and that the inherent difficulty of the task increases under a republican government. Nevertheless, we have been unsuccessful even far beyond all precedent in our establishment of a police.

Our federal police is, in point of fact, merely a private detective agency for revenue and postal purposes, having all the odious features of secrecy and espionage about it without any protection to life or property, and lacking all the essential elements of proper organization and supervision. It has thus become open to the most scandalous abuses; gangs of counterfeiters, mail-robbers, etc., notoriously buying off detectives, to let them carry on, undenounced, their criminal occupations.

The States themselves have no police system at all, and rely altogether upon private or municipal corporations to do that which is essentially the duty of the State. This deficiency leaves of course all the smaller cities, villages, and agricultural districts open to the unchecked violence and villainy of the thief, robber, and murderer; for only large cities can afford police forces, and private police corporations find it profitable to carry on their business only in large cities. Hence the terrible crimes in the country districts that so often startle the community, the assassinations, the rapes, the robberies, the horse-stealing, that surprise us where one would least expect them. Such horrible tragedies as the Benders perpetrated in Kansas—who came unknown, settled down on a lonely tract of land, and built upon it a small log tavern, butchering almost every day some unsuspecting traveler that came in for rest or refreshment—should not be possible to happen at all in a well-organized state. No state can possibly protect its citizens in their lives, liberty, and property that thus permits everybody to settle down anywhere without knowledge of their real names, former residence, character, or occupation. The issue is simply this: whether we shall continue to expose our lives and property to constant danger, or submit to some slight inconveniences that are absolutely necessary to avert that danger.

II.

The police of municipal corporations, finally, the only legal police we have, has grown up in such an unsystematic fragmentary sort of way as to be in one respect singularly inefficient, and in another oppressively tyrannical. It has neither the powers it ought to have, nor is it debarred from exercising the powers it ought not to have. Policemen have shot down—brutally murdered—men simply for not obeying their call to halt; while on the other hand they allow the most flagrant vice and crime to ply their shameful crimes in the open streets. Horse-cars, omnibuses, and other vehicles run over and kill hundreds of people yearly in our large cities; other hundreds break their limbs or necks in walking public streets that are wholly insecure; and wild cattle, running loose or driven through the public thoroughfares of our cities, gore men, women, and children nearly every day; the police all the while looking on unconcernedly, while wasting time and attention by making raids on gambling-houses and dragging the lowest classes of loafers and harlots before a police magistrate for a periodical fine.

To remedy this state of affairs it will be absolutely necessary to establish for every State a thorough police force, under the direction of a chief department specially created for that purpose. This organization should have its representatives in every township of the State, in every village, and in every block of a large city, all in constant rapport with each other. It should have abundant power to carry out its objects, and yet be sufficiently checked, not wantonly to interfere with men's lawful rights and liberties.

From such a police organization all features of secrecy and mystery should be strictly excluded. No operation of the state should need a mask or require concealment. The state has an absolute right to demand of each citizen his name, antecedents, occupation, character, and residence. It is an utter impossibility that the state should be able to meet its obligation to protect every citizen unless this right is conceded.

III.

It must, therefore, be made absolutely impossible that any person can arrive at and take up his quarters in any township or village, or in any part of a city, unless the police are immediately advised of the fact of his arrival, his name, residence, occupation, and proposed destination. If it is found necessary that a system of passports is indispensable to secure this object, such a system should be at once introduced. The notion of passports may seem very objectionable to us nowadays; but really, when calmly considered, the passport system does not infringe on our individual liberty of intercommunication to any serious extent, while it certainly affords it fuller protection than could be realized by any other measure.

Surely every citizen of a state desires freedom to go to any part of that state, and be protected on the way against violence and fraud. But how can the state protect him when its police are unacquainted with the names, occupations, and destinations of all other citizens with whom he may come in contact? Hence he himself and all others must be made subject to some measure that shall effectually make it possible for the state to obtain that knowledge whenever needed, and no measure is so adequate for this purpose as the passport.

If the name passport is held objectionable, some other name can easily be invented, and the instrument itself can be rearranged with the application of modern science, so as to take away from it all the features that formerly made it odious. A small printed card, with the photograph on one side, and the name, occupation, age, and residence of the owner, leaving the necessary blanks to be filled, on the other side, and the seal of office affixed, with the date of issue, would serve all purposes, and could easily be secured against counterfeiting.

Such a passport system can, moreover, be very readily combined with the existing registration system for voters, making the latter far more adequate to subserve its purposes. It is a notorious fact that under the present system of registration fraudulent votes are cast at every election. People vote who have no right to vote; others vote two, three, or more times at the same election; and the police are powerless to prevent the outrage. Nobody knows all the men who offer their votes; neither their name, their occupation, nor their residence.

IV.

Under such a system as I propose it would be impossible for the murderers, house-burners, forgers, and other criminals that prey upon society, to carry on their nefarious trades unperceived. Nor would such a system of passports and registration allow the sudden vanishing of men from our midst, no one knowing when, where, or how they vanish. What unknown, dreadful crimes may envelop the many inexplicable sudden disappearances of well-known persons from the midst of their friends! But a short time ago a woman was found dead in her house in New York, *five weeks* having elapsed since her death or murder, and her body too decomposed to show whether murder had been committed or not! Ought such an occurrence to be possible under proper police administration?

What carelessness, again, is more culpable than that which permits our boats and ships to leave their harbors without rendering a full list of their passengers? How many families linger in agony when the news of a shipwreck is borne to them, and no list of the ship's passengers can be obtained anywhere! How many persons plunge annually from our steamboats into the waters of our rivers and lakes, no one knowing their name or residence! How many unknown individuals are killed annually on our railroads, no railroad company keeping a list of its passengers, their names, residences, or destinations!

A well-considered system of passports and registration would speedily put an end to this state of things, and amply repay, by the benefits conferred in personal security of ourselves, our friends, and relatives, for the first slight annoyances it might give occasion to; and it would have the additional advantage of protecting every holder of such a passport against the unjustifiable annoyance to which men are subject from the police under the present loose system. The violation of the rights of personal liberty and security in one's own house against police entrance and search would no longer be possible; and to the additional security conferred would thus be added far greater protection against unjustifiable, illegal, and despotic acts of the present irresponsible police administrations in the cities.

DOMESTIC RELATIONS.

CHAPTER I.

MARRIAGE.

NATURE has separated the human race, for the purpose of its perpetuation, into sexes, the union of which has thus become the most important event of human life. In one way or another every form of legislation has attempted to regulate this union, but in no instance of history, except the monogamic code of Moses, has this regulation proceeded from rational principles. It has always been based on traditional notions, and existing facts and prejudices. Nevertheless, it is of infinite importance to the state, for on this union depends the transmission of name and property, and therefore it is one of the main factors in the realization of man's freedom and self-determination.

The reason why legislation has blundered more in its attempts to regulate the union of the sexes than in almost any other field is to be found in the fact that it has confounded the moral with the legal point of view. From a moral point of view, the woman is, in the union of the sexes, the passive element, her whole activity centering in love, that is, in the surrendering of herself to the chosen one. She cannot have any other active motive without debasing herself in her own eyes, as well as in the eyes of all others, without, indeed, what has been so emphatically termed prostituting herself. The male, on the contrary, seeks the woman. He is not actuated by such love,—meaning love to signify the surrendering of one's self to another for that other's sake,—and could not have that motive without debasing himself and the woman also. No man can surrender himself to a woman with the self-conscious motive to gratify her, without the utmost degradation, whereas woman needs that very motive to retain her self-esteem. This is the peculiarity of the moral relation between the sexes, and more or less typified in all physical phenomena, as well as recognized by universal public opinion.

It has been the mistake of the lawgivers to take cognizance of this moral relation and apply it in the operation of the law, where it necessarily assumed a different shape, altogether wrong and unjust. In the moral world the woman does not take lower rank, because her whole activity in the union of the sexes is love, nor man higher rank, because his activity is primarily passionate: both are in all respects equal, each acting according to her and his organization. But under the conception of law, which cannot take cognizance of love, the passiveness of the woman placed her in a subordinate position, and thus it chanced that legislation did not recognize woman as the equal of man. Hence the most absurd laws regarding matrimony, the relation between the sexes, the property of women, and inheritance; laws that have been, and are still, the disgrace of mankind, and which were imposed upon woman without her consent.

I propose to consider these matters on purely rational grounds, without regard to traditional notions and prejudices.

It is clear that the law should make no distinction whatever between man and woman while they are single, or between men and widows. In all matters of property, personal right, and political position, the law should apply equally to both sexes, and secure to each the power to realize the greatest good and happiness from the fit and harmonious exercise of all the faculties of their minds and bodies.

It is also apparent that a legislation which deprives woman of her personality during marriage is barbarous, and, moreover, absurd where such legislation allows divorces; for, if the marriage merged the woman's personality into that of the man, how could any subsequent declaration of law separate that personality again? It may be logical enough that the church, which assumes to legislate according to the moral law, should entertain this view of having the wife's personality once and forever joined with that of the husband; but it was a strange lapse of rational procedure that the common law, which pretends to look upon marriage as a civil contract, should have retained a like conception so utterly at variance with this its fundamental principle. No man loses his personality by entering into a civil contract. Why, then, should a woman lose hers? In her moral consciousness she may thus submerge hers, and may be bound to do so; but no government, unless it become theocratic and a hierarchy, can consider this view of internal morality, or legislate concerning it.

The government is not to apply the moral law, which addresses itself purely to the individual, but simply to furnish the means of its fullest realization, by empowering each citizen of the state to attain the greatest good, happiness, and wisdom for himself and others.

Hence the law must place man and woman in all respects on a footing of perfect equality, and secure to the married woman the same rights of personality which are claimed for the husband. The law, regarding marriage purely as a civil contract for a specific purpose, should be advised of the fact that the contract is made, and of its conditions, if there be any. Hence every such contract should be recorded in the proper public office, and every failure so to record it should subject the husband to a fine.

But in the absence of any written or other evidence of marriage, the cohabitation of a man and woman as husband and wife should constitute marriage; and the simple cohabitation of man and woman, by living together in the same house, occupying the same apartments, and deporting themselves as if they were married, should also constitute marriage in fact, whereby both parties would be estopped from denying the existence of the marriage. The law should always, in such cases of cohabitation, presume marriage to exist, to suppress prostitution and seduction as far as practicable.

Concerning the conditions of marriage contracts where they exist, they must be carried out according to their intent and meaning, but they should apply only to property or rights then existing; as to all gains, earnings, and profits during marriage, they should be disposed of according to the principles of the Code Napoleon, and no marriage contract should affect them, except in cases of divorce. The law of copartnership would apply, with the exception, that in case of marriage the relation must continue during life, or until the termination of it by a decree of divorce. Any other rule would render it impossible for the law to provide for the children, by regulating the transmission of property and inheritance, which should be regulated in accordance with a code requiring the descent to the right heirs of the deceased party, according to their degrees of consanguinity, so as to limit all devises to others to one-sixth or one-tenth of the estate descending in such cases. No parent should be permitted by law to exclude his children born in lawful wedlock from their inheritance, except in cases of gross ingratitude or rebellion against just and legal parental authority.

Divorces should be granted, where both parties consent, if proper provisions are made for the husband, wife, and children, and approved by the court. If either party objects to the divorce, the question should be decided by the court according to justice and equity under all the circumstances of the case; but whenever it is manifest that a fatal disagreement or incompatibility of temper exists between the parties, the divorce should be granted, for the marriage has no longer any real existence when love has fled and a divorce is applied for. All marriage contracts should provide for the disposition of all the property belonging to the community, and to either party prior to the marriage, in case of a divorce being decreed by the court, so that on the happening of such an event the contract would govern in the division of the estates, unless special equities were shown to exist.

Where both parties consent to a divorce and the marriage contract provides for the disposition of the property and the children, upon the happening of such an event, the divorce should be decreed without any proofs, or examination into the circumstances, as a matter of course. But if either party consenting to the divorce should set up any special equitable circumstances or claims to the property or the custody of the children, in contravention of the terms of the ante-nuptial contract, the court should determine them when the divorce is granted.

No disability of either party, for contracting any future marriage, should ever be decreed on granting a divorce, unless it appears from the evidence on the hearing that the guilty party is of unsound mind, or of a cruel and barbarous nature, dangerous to human liberty or life; in which case, such guilty party may be forever barred from contracting another marriage.

In case of lunacy or insanity of one of the parties to the marriage, if such lunacy or insanity becomes incurable, and is so found by a jury, the other party to the marriage should be able to obtain a decree of divorce on condition of providing for and securing a reasonable support for life of the lunatic or insane person.

If the parties contracting marriage do not desire a divorce from the bonds of matrimony, but from any cause determine to live separate and apart from each other, and cannot agree to a division of their property between them, and as to the custody of the children, they should be permitted to apply to the court for a decree to determine their just rights and equities under all the circumstances of their case.

If either party compels the other, in such case, to abandon the homestead, residence, or place of abode of husband and wife, the injured party should be permitted to apply to the court for a reasonable support and maintenance during any such period, or for life.

In all cases of divorce for impotency, the court may decree the party demanding a divorce for such reason to support the other party during life.

The rule of law in general copartnerships is, that each partner is responsible for the debts and liabilities of the firm of which he is a member, and this rule should apply to the relation of husband and wife during marriage, if there is no contract. There should be a unity of interests in this relation during its continuance, except only so far as this may be changed by ante-nuptial contracts.

Marriage being a civil contract made under the law, or sanctioned by it when it exists *de facto*, the state should determine the age for its consummation, the disabilities that should prevent or annul it, and the impediments to its existence between certain persons. The act should be the unbiased, deliberate resolve of the parties; no other influence but pure, disinterested love should prompt it, and both parties should know precisely in what legal relation they will thereafter stand to each other. Each party should be free from all disorders of a hereditary character, or otherwise tending to shorten life or to afflict the children that may be born of the marriage, and all possible precautions should be taken to prevent the matrimonial union of diseased or unsound persons.

It is, however, the interest of the state, as the only effective remedy against prostitution and seduction, that reasonably early marriages should be encouraged. Under such a system of schools as I have proposed, whereby every pupil will be educated for a vocation in life, and the means to earn a living, the contracting parties would both be able to do so, and early marriages would become the rule instead of the exception. The chief obstacles to marriage in early life are, the uncertainty of the bridegroom that he will be able to make a living, and a fear that the girl whom he intends to make his wife may not have the ability or inclination to conduct their new household on economical principles. It is somewhat singular that the extravagant mode of living in our free country should in this way place the same restraint upon our marriages, which in many countries of Europe interpose to prevent them. There the poor young people, who would gladly marry and be content jointly to face the future by the exercise of industry and economy, are met by the interference of government, in some form or other, lest they or their offspring should become a burden to the community; here the young withhold from marriage because they themselves contemplate this result. The consequence, in Europe, is a cohabitation of the couple without the marriage ceremony, a state of things already so common in Vienna that legalized marriages among the poor are the exception. In our own country the result has been an increase of prostitution, which is surely undermining the health, morality, and happiness of the people.

My system of schools proposes to check the growth of this evil at its very root by furnishing to every man and woman of the country an education for a vocation that will always secure him or her a livelihood, and also teaching every woman how to conduct a household in the most economical way, and carry it on upon safe business principles.

This would also check the tendency in some women to extravagance, and living beyond the legitimate means of their husbands' incomes, which is the ruin of so many business men, who are often led into hazardous ventures and reckless speculations in order to gratify the extravagant tastes of proud, idle, or vain wives

As the system of law herein proposed will become the surest bulwark of defense against the enslavement of woman, under the different forms of despotism that have hitherto oppressed her, it is especially the duty of woman to aid the establishment of this system of government by all the means in her power, and particularly by setting such an example of economy, industry, self-sacrifice, frugality, and temperance, in all things in the household and in society, as will show her to be worthy of that full equality with man under the laws to which this system would elevate her.

It will become the duty of the federal government to establish the monogamic system of marriage as a universal rule in the States of the republic. This can be accomplished only by an amendment of the Constitution of the United States for that purpose, prohibiting in all parts of the republic that polygamy which has already raised its poisonous crest in Utah, and is beginning to show its demoralizing effects as the Chinese immigration increases. Polygamy is the foundation-stone of all the Asiatic despotisms, and under its corruptions the female sex has everywhere sunk to a depth of slavery and degradation almost inconceivable. Human liberty and free governments are wholly incompatible with polygamy or prostitution in any form.

It will appear from the foregoing that I claim for every individual, male or female, the same position of political rights and equality in the state, the husband always representing the head of the family, according to natural laws. This should be no new claim to those who have examined the history of our race. That eminent English jurist, Sir Henry Maine, has shown most conclusively, in his recent Oxford lectures, that woman, in early history, did occupy that very station to which the advocates of free representative governments now seek to elevate her again. Through the Roman law, the Hindu law, and the laws of Western Europe, all these being branches of the original law of the Aryan race, he has traced the same original notion of the full equality of the sexes. There is no doubt that the separate property of the wife was conceded by the old Hindu laws far more thoroughly than it is even now by most of the states of modern Europe.

The influence of the hierarchical teachings of Brahma, combined with the spread of polygamic practices, has gradually lowered the position of women in the Orient below that even of the slave, while in our own civilization woman has passed through the reverential phase of chivalry—which assigned to her a romantically exalted station—to her present condition of almost absolute equality with man. It now only remains to secure to her this rational condition for all time, on proper principles, so as to perpetuate our free institutions upon the solid foundations of universal suffrage and political equality for all men and women, in their triune characteristics of knowledge, wealth, and individuality.

CHAPTER II.

CHILDREN.

THE children are to become the future citizens of the state, and upon their proper education and development the ultimate success of our free republican institutions depends. The addition to our population arises from natural increase or immigration from foreign countries.

Hitherto immigration has been allowed to flow into our States from every quarter, without any proper restriction or supervision; and it has already become manifest that no State can safely continue this policy without subjecting its citizens to all kinds of demoralizing, hierarchical, and corrupting influences. The federal government alone can regulate this matter, and it is the plain duty of Congress to pass laws preventing the immigration of slaves, criminals, vagrants, pauper children, and other vagabonds, the human wrecks of despotic civilizations. Of the wretched pauper and orphan children the state should assert its right to educate and provide for them at the public expense; and as for the children of citizens or foreigners born here, it is of the greatest interest to the state that they should receive the best education practicable, and be perfected in the department of life they may choose for their respective vocations. The system of schools, hereinbefore described, would furnish the means to accomplish this beneficent object, and increase the value and usefulness of the generation growing up under it more than a hundred-fold, and diminish crime and immorality in the same proportion.

But the question arises, will the parents take advantage of these public means for education, and send their children to the state schools? The child naturally belongs to the parents, who are its natural protectors and instructors. Nature gave them offspring to educate and fit them for active life. The right of parents to control these children and exercise just authority over them cannot be questioned, and for this reason the state has no right to compel parents to send them to the public schools. In all these matters there should be no compulsion. The schools, proposed to be established, would necessarily be the best, for all purposes of general and special instruction, ever founded in any age of the world; but private schools may be founded upon the same plan and carried on, or the existing schools of all kinds may be remodeled and reformed, so as to carry out the same objects. Though this would involve an unnecessary expense to parties undertaking the enterprise for private or sectarian purposes, the right of doing so would be unquestionable.

Nevertheless, there is no doubt that a large majority of the children in the state, especially in the agricultural districts, would attend the state public schools, and whenever a child over the age of ten years should appeal for education and admission to the state schools, and it should appear that its parents do not educate it, then it should be admitted, maintained if necessary, and taught at the public expense. Children having no known parents or whose parents have died, leaving them destitute, should be maintained and educated at the public expense for a vocation. So also the children who may be abandoned by their parents, guardians, or protectors, should be placed under the guardianship of the state and educated. In like manner all children who are sent out by their parents to beg, in any guise, or to become outcasts, thieves, or vagrants in society, should be placed under the guardianship of the state and educated.

In order to provide for the better moral training and management of all such children, a system should be adopted to place them with families in the rural districts, having few or no children of their own, so that they might be adopted if possible, and where they could attend the common and agricultural schools and enjoy the benefit of domestic care and instruction, at the expense of the state, which, in the majority of instances, would be very trifling, as the child after twelve years of age would generally be able to earn its own living, without interfering with its proper education for the vocation of a farmer or for other business. If such children should prove to have great intellectual powers, they should not be limited to any special vocation, but might pass on to the highest schools and the university.

No partiality or favoritism should be shown in the examination or grading of the scholars in any school, but true merit and excellence, without regard to any extraneous circumstances of position, family, or wealth of parents, should be the only criterion for the advancement of scholars to the various grades of schools. Thus the system of education would be made to harmonize with the theory upon which the government is based, and the scholars would learn the principles of justice, morality, equality, liberty, and law as they progressed in their studies.

In all cases of criminal acts by children under fifteen years of age, the reformatory measures should be arranged with as little exposure or publicity as possible. The present mode of dealing with children criminals is simply barbarous and immoral, resulting in dishonor and unnecessary expense to the state. All children who may become wards of the state should have every protection and advancement they may need, and they should be treated in the schools with the same regard, kindness, and attention as any other scholars.

All the sanitary measures and moral instruction recommended in this work should be fully carried out, and practiced in all the schools to be established or hereafter to be brought within the scope of the system herein proposed, so that the graduate of either of the schools will pass into the scenes of active life as fully prepared to meet all its trials and vicissitudes as practicable. His certificate of graduation would be a letter of credit upon the world of intelligence and practical activity, that must insure him a livelihood and independence if he be diligent, prudent, and frugal.

CONCLUSION.

Thus far in the progress of my work, for the amendment and greater perfection of the governmental organizations in each State, I have pointed out the affirmative duties of a free state to protect the bodies of its citizens from physical disease and weakness; their minds from ignorance and superstition; and their personal and commercial intercommunication from all forms of tyranny, unjust taxation, and oppression, by providing systems of public hygiene, public education, and public intercommunication, to be enforced in all essential particulars by the affirmative exercise of the sovereign power of the people, expressed through a state organization, whereby all citizens,—men, women, and children,—in the state will be protected and secured in the fit and harmonious use of all their faculties of mind and body, to the end that each one may attain and enjoy the greatest good, happiness, wisdom, and perfection of which his faculties are capable, and whereby all the co-operative benefits of a rational system of government, providing for the common enjoyment of the same blessings by each family and the whole society of the state,—free from the existing obstructions of superstition, tyranny, monopolies, prerogative, caste, aristocracies, and all other irrational and unjust schemes to elevate one person by debasing another, will be forever secured to the people.

The state will thus become the fountain from which all the blessings a good government can bestow upon the people will continually flow, increasing the happiness, enjoyment, and prosperity of all, and attracting the love and gratitude of all good persons to itself, to secure the perpetuation of its organic life and usefulness.

To preserve the common liberties and franchises of the people, and prevent official frauds, peculation and partisan despotism, I have suggested a federal, State, and municipal system of newspaper publication, whereby the people will be enabled to detect and prevent them. The bane of an unbridled and corrupt press will find its sure antidote in accurate official newspapers; and these impartial publications may serve as useful a purpose as the serpent of brass set up by Moses in the land of Edom, in looking upon which the bites of the fiery serpents were healed that God sent in the wilderness of Mount Hor, to sting and poison the Israelites for their sins.

I have also proposed the establishment of a national currency of Treasury legal-tender notes, receivable for all debts and duties, to the exclusion of all other money, at par, in the trade and industries of the republic, to be issued in sufficient quantity to redeem all the 5-20 bonds now outstanding, say, one billion seven hundred million dollars, upon the passage of an act of Congress authorizing this to be done, and requiring the bonds to be presented at the Treasury for redemption in national money, on or before a certain day, after which time no further interest would be demandable or paid. This would save to the people one hundred million dollars annual interest in coin, now paid on those bonds, that were sold at currency prices, and at the same time supply a national money circulation, now actually required to carry on the vast and growing industries and trade of the country. The objection that such money is irredeemable has no validity, since our own experience has shown that the inferior legal-tender currency, not receivable for duties, needed no other redemption than to be receivable at par, as it now is, for all articles for sale in the United States. Money is only a vehicle, a medium for trade and business. It needs only to be made current by law, as Treasury notes are now; and the government has already established its lawful power to make the national currency current money throughout the republic. Since the national money of an inferior grade has answered this purpose thoroughly for ten years past, a complete legal-tender currency will serve us now and hereafter, though it were quadrupled by the redemption of the 5-20 bonds. There is no other way, in my opinion, to meet our financial embarrassments created by the acts of Congress of 1869–70, subjecting us to the coin despotism. There is no other way to liquidate the national debt, and this will do so, fully and justly. It is a public necessity to adopt this plan, which will meet no opposition, except from bondholders, national banks, and money-monopolies; and even these are really interested to favor it, if the national debt cannot otherwise be paid. The success of this policy would free us at once from enormous burdens, crushing and crippling all branches of trade and industry. It would enable the government very soon to reduce the federal taxes and tariff seventy-five per cent., and cause the latter in a few years to cease altogether, when free trade, the greatest boon to a free people, would shower its glorious blessings upon all industries, productions, trade, and commerce.

It is not practicable for any individual to accomplish this great task I have proposed to myself, and some of my plans may be more or less imperfect; and, indeed, all methods of government, invented by man, will always suggest further reforms and amendments, for the securing of still greater good, happiness, wisdom, and inspiration to our race. It is the greatest virtue of this plan, that it provides in its educational system for its own improvement and perfection in all respects, as future experience may suggest; and I submit this work to the careful study of the people of the United States and of other countries, if it may be deemed worthy of such consideration. It is my ardent hope and desire that any one who believes he can improve upon it, or invent another system for working out more perfectly the beneficent results contemplated by me, will present his method to the public for examination.

THE END.

www.ingramcontent.com/pod-product-compliance
Lightning Source LLC
LaVergne TN
LVHW010242110826
845151LV00004B/1363

* 9 7 8 1 4 2 5 5 2 3 8 6 2 *